Sources of Funding for Ireland's Entrepreneurs

Cecilia Hegarty
&
Howard Frederick

Leona,

Best Wishes

Cecilia

Availability: This book is available at major bookstores on the Island of Ireland.

About Cecilia Hegarty

Dr Cecilia B Hegarty is a Teaching Fellow with the Northern Ireland Centre for Entrepreneurship (NICENT) where she advises the Science and Engineering Faculties on how to implement Northern Ireland's entrepreneurship agenda in third level education.

Cecilia has lectured and examined within Dublin Institute of Technology, Dublin for approximately three years and established the first Faculty web interface to assist placement students and business owners in learning about business. Her entrepreneurship teachings, in particular, have been applied as far a field as Rotorua, New Zealand.

She has acted as a consultant on different projects including EU 5th Framework project to improve integration and *embeddedness* in the lagging rural regions of Europe. She continues to play an active role in training events for practitioners and in showcasing enterprise development to foreign delegations. Her pioneering all-island research involving 2,697 entrepreneurs in Northern Ireland and the Republic of Ireland formed part of her PhD research into entrepreneurial development in micro enterprises and SMEs in the service industries.

Although a primary graduate of University of Ulster, Cecilia was also a business student at University of Indianapolis, Indiana. Cecilia has had numerous full paper publications at diverse (entrepreneurship, tourism innovation, geography, rural and research) conferences as well as journals, book contributions and reviews. Cecilia is the first Teaching Fellow to be seconded from the University to pilot entrepreneurship education and training programmes at regional level. She has also undertaken the role of promotions manager and conference organiser for NICENT and has been on the board for curriculum development and a mentor for students with emergent technology projects.

About Howard Frederick

Howard H. Frederick (BA, Stanford), MA (San Francisco State U), PhD (The American University), New Zealand Institute of Directors.

A Stanford graduate with broad European, Latin American, and Australasian experience, Prof Frederick is recognized as an authority in the field of ICT, business innovation, and economic growth. He is the author of New Zealand's first *Knowledge Economy* report (1999), the *Global Entrepreneurship Monitor New Zealand* reports as well as of numerous articles and books.

Howard is New Zealand's only Professor of Innovation & Entrepreneurship, based at the School of Management & Entrepreneurship at Unitec New Zealand, where he teaches Global Market Entry, e-Business, New Business Environment, Market Research, and Political Communication. He is Senior Scholar at the Leonard Greif Center for Entrepreneurial Management of the Marshall School of Businesses, University of Southern California, USA. He is also the rare European who lectures in Maori Leadership for the School of Maori Education.

He is on the board of four start-ups in New Zealand. After the Fall of the Berlin Wall, Frederick launched a dot.com high-tech start-up in the eastern German State of Saxony called the Saxony Telematics Development Corporation. He had eleven employees and a multi-million German mark budget. When he tried to privatise the state-owned shares, he was deposed as CEO and came to a more business-friendly country. Prof Frederick's current commercial activities focus on Ten3 New Zealand Limited www.ten3.co.nz.

Note: Already we have produced *Sources of Funding* for entrepreneurs in New Zealand, Australia, and Ireland. We are looking for co-authors for other countries. If you are interested, please contact hfrederick@ten3.co.nz

Table of Contents

List of Tables

List of Figures

Foreword

Your book felt like a meal at a fancy restaurant – the portions are small and what you get is quality! That's what one of our first readers said about this book. That reminded us of a job advertisement we once saw:

> WANTED: ENTREPRENEUR. *Immediate opening.* Exciting, exhausting, high-risk position. Must have the ability to discover new business opportunities, discern market needs, and match with appropriate solutions before they become obvious to others. Applicant must be willing to invest hard work and create effort before others recognise the merit of their ideas. Ability to work with financial institutions, investors, and venture capitalists to attract financial backing will be essential for upward mobility in the position. Pay will be very poor for failure and very good for success.[1]

"Attracting financial backing will be essential". Entrepreneurs don't have a lot of time and yet they have many urgent needs. In turn, the world has always been and always will be in desperate need of entrepreneurs. They take a brilliant idea and make a flourishing business out of it. They are the lifeblood of the economy because they create new wealth.

That's why we've written this easily digestible book for the Island of Ireland. It's packed with information condensed down to a form that you can consume easily about how to attract that financial backing.

Entrepreneurship is what has made many nations great historically. To help our entrepreneurs succeed today, we need to create an environment in which the next generation of entrepreneurs will pick up the challenge, and grow the wealth back into this country for the benefit of themselves and for our people as a whole.

It is our hope that this small book will motivate the many people who articulate the value of entrepreneurship to ask the next set of questions and do something about them so that we all benefit from their energy and efforts. This book is a great starting point for those who are up to the challenge!

Cecilia Hegarty & Howard Frederick, July 2006

M oney is like a sixth sense without which you cannot make complete use of the other five".

William Somerset Maugham, *Of Human Bondage*

Objectives

- To understand the funding environment for start-up ventures across the island of Ireland

- To know the easiest ways to bootstrap your business and get start-up financing

- To differentiate between debt and equity as methods of financing

- To examine commercial loans and public stock offerings as sources of capital

- To discuss private placements as an opportunity for equity capital

- To study the market for venture capital and to review venture capitalists' evaluation criteria for new ventures

- To discuss the importance of evaluating venture capitalists for a "best fit" selection

- To examine the existing informal risk-capital market (including "angel capital")

- To describe sources of venture capital, private equity and government funding available in the Irish context.

Introduction

It is often said that if entrepreneurs are the engines that drive new companies, then financing is the fuel that propels them. The best sources of funding for the newest firms in Ireland and Northern Ireland are bootstrapping (creative ways of launching a business); informal investment (financial contributions from family, friends, and colleagues); and government funding programmes. Formal or 'classic' venture capital funds (including business angels) is usually reserved for companies that are already on a high growth track. Beyond this, the growth-oriented entrepreneur will rely heavily on bank loans and other more traditional sources of funding.

What exactly are these sources of funding and what is expected of an entrepreneur seeking to secure these funds?

It is important to understand not only the various sources of funding, but also the expectations and requirements of these sources. Without this understanding, an entrepreneur may be frustrated with attempts to find appropriate start-up financing.

Studies have investigated the various sources of finance preferred by entrepreneurs.[2] Table 1 outlines some of the most significant sources of finance that entrepreneurs will pursue. These sources range from debt to equity depending upon the type of financing that is arranged. As illustrated in Figure 1, entrepreneurs have a number of sources of capital that correspond to the venture's stage of development. Notice that the level of risk and the stage of the firm's development impact the appropriate source of financing for the entrepreneurial ventures.

In this guide book we examine the various sources of capital available to new ventures, with some insights into the approach required of the entrepreneur. Start-up entrepreneurs have different needs from growing entrepreneurs, so we first start with sources of start-up finance and then go on to look at ways to finance growing companies.

Table 1 Sources of Entrepreneurial Finance[3]

Source	Approach
Bank Loans	Redeemable preferred stock
Community banks	The wide world of the Internet
The (self) chosen few	Public Equity
Asset-backed borrowing	Investment- or commercial-banking links
Micro-loans	Corporate Support
Third-party loan guarantees	Strategic partnerships
Venture leasing	International Finance
Credit cards	Financing international accounts receivable
Online credit search engines	International strategic partnerships
Family and Friends	The Right Contacts
Tapping personal ties	Capital intermediaries
Asset sales	Entrepreneurship programs
Private Equity	Performance-oriented, flexible terms

Figure 1 Finance over the life of an entrepreneurial firm [4]

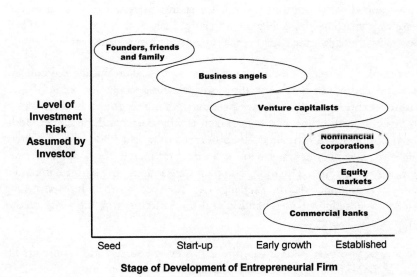

Bootstrapping your business

Bootstrapping is a means of financing a small firm through highly creative acquisition and use of resources without raising equity from traditional sources or borrowing money from a bank. *Bootstrapping means starting a new business without start-up finance.* It offers many advantages for entrepreneurs and, aside from getting money from friends and family, is probably the best method to get an entrepreneurial firm operating and well-positioned to seek debt financing from banks or equity finance from outside investors at a later time.

Bootstrapping relies greatly on networks, trust, cooperation, and wise use of the firm's existing resources, rather than going into debt or giving away equity. Have a hard look at your firm's financial position. Sometimes financing is not even needed. One quarter of the Inc 500 (*Inc. Magazine's* annual list of its 500 US small business start-ups) began with less than $5,000, half with less than $25,000 and three quarters with less than $100,000.

Here are the main bootstrapping tips: Look for the "low-hanging fruit". Use a copycat idea. Find quick, break-even, cash-generating products. Firms that are already making money build credibility in the eyes of investors. Meanwhile, keep growth in check. Too many start-ups fail because they grow beyond their financial means. Focus on cash (not on profits, market share, or anything else). Because of their financial means, bootstrapped firms cannot afford to pursue a number of strategic goals. For example, bootstrapped firms cannot pursue loss-making strategies to build a market share or a customer base. Having a healthy cash flow is critical to survival, thus sales strategies must ensure healthy returns from the outset.

Ever think of barter? The Bartercard network has taken the age-old concept of barter and added flexibility, allowing a business to pay for some of their business expenses with their own products. Members go out of their way to do business with other members, which is why Bartercard guarantees additional business. An estimated 20-25 percent of world trade is now barter.[5] The most basic barter transaction is a direct exchange of goods or services between two entities. The more complex transactions that barter companies have developed include: the exchange of trade credits for under-performing assets, remarketing of merchandise and the retirement of the trade credits for goods and services.

Of course, you need to cultivate the banks even before you become creditworthy. Bank financing is usually unavailable to start-up firms, especially if little or no collateral is offered. However, bank financing is quite important for small firms once they are established and making some profit. Even bootstrappers need to keep good books, immaculate records, and sound balance sheets from day one. This allows you to approach your banker with confidence once the firm has been in operation for a few years and is creditworthy. Don't forget to check if the Irish League of Credit Unions could offer you a small loan to get your business started, many small villages conveniently have local branches and you can deal with someone you know.

Bootstrapping methods vary with the venture's development stage: firms in rapid stage growth are more likely to focus on minimizing capital by reducing operations cost.[6] In highly risky and high tech environments, bootstrap financing techniques such as delayed payments are often preferred.[7]

Bootstrapping techniques[8]

Bootstrapping options for product development

- Prepaid licenses, royalties, or advances from customers

- Special deals on access to product hardware

- Development of product at night and on weekends while working elsewhere

- Customer-funded research and development

- Turning a consultant project into a commercial product

- Least useful methods here are research grants and university-based research incubators.

Bootstrapping options for business development

- Foregone, delayed or reduced compensation

- Working from home using personal savings

- Deals with professional service providers at below-competitive rates

- Space at below-market or very low rent

- Personal credit cards and home equity loans

- Least useful here are severance payments, barter, and special terms with customers.

Bootstrapping options to minimize the need for capital

- Buy used equipment instead of new

- Borrow equipment from other businesses for short-term projects or rent short-term incubation space

- Use interest on overdue payments from customers

- Hire personnel for shorter periods instead of employing permanently

- Coordinate purchases with other businesses (mutual purchasing of goods)

- Lease equipment instead of buying

- Cease business relations with customers who frequently pay late

- Offer same conditions to all customers (no preferential treatment)

- Buy on consignment or trade credit from suppliers

- Deliberately choose customers who pay quickly

- Share business premises with others or run business out of your house

- Employ relatives or friends at non-market salaries

- Least useful are sharing of equipment and employees employed with other local businesses.

Bootstrapping options to meet the need for capital

- Withhold your own salary payment for short or long period of time

- Pay employees with company stock (give employees some ownership)

- Seek out best purchasing conditions with suppliers

- Deliberately delay payment to suppliers

- Use your private credit card for business expenses

- Obtain loans from relatives and friends

- Barter underused products or services with other firms

- Franchise or license the product or business idea to others for a royalty fee

- The least employed methods here include raising capital from a factoring company (through selling the firm's accounts receivable) and obtaining central or state subsidies.

Cheap ways to bootstrap your business[9]

Build-out Allowances from Landlords – Banks will often allow you to count build-out allowances as capital in your source and use of funds statement. While the money comes in and goes out, it does increase the overall cash flow and size of your deal.

Vertical Integration – Capital can often be raised from outside companies with a vested interest in developing either distribution channels, or assuring themselves of adequate product flow from cash-starved companies. Example: a distributor invested in his supplier to assure adequate inventory.

Professionals Associated with the Business – Present a way for investors to be more profitable in their own companies through the proposed investment. Law firms, advertising agencies, executive recruiters and professional consultants will often accept partial payment in stock, warrants or options in return for services. This is an excellent way to build a powerful team of professionals with a vested interest in your success and your success in raising capital. Many of these professionals are also angel investors, who can champion your cause with other private investors.

White Knights – If you are a retailer with poor credit, and cannot get merchandise shipped without direct payment, have someone with better credit buy the products and resell to you. You may pay the White Knight a few percentage points each month. If you have a high turnover ratio, it will allow you to re-establish cash flow and credit. A few specialists handle these types of operations, but you can find them through factoring companies.

Technical or Professional Expertise – Many professionals are willing to reduce their fees in exchange for equity, e.g. 1 percent for €10,000 of work on a start-up company valued at €100,000. Although the services will not be totally free, they will usually be reduced by about 50 percent. You may even be able to arrange options or warrants to avoid initial dilution. Plus, you can provide the professional with an exit strategy prior to an IPO, if another large investor enters your market.

Sell Licenses or Marketing Rights – Selling off rights to foreign or geographic markets, or private labelling products, is an excellent vehicle for young companies. You can use both exclusive and non-exclusive arrangements. All methods should have some type of quota and non-competition clauses. The downside is that later investors may feel that you have sold off too much of the potential, so they will not invest as readily.

Finding informal investment

When first-time entrepreneurs look for capital, they sometimes don't realise that most start-up funding for new ventures doesn't usually come from banks or venture capitalists. It comes from the 4F's—friends, family, founders and other "foolhardy investors" (plus neighbours, work colleagues, and even strangers). We call them "informal investors".

Informal investors use their own money and carry out their own (sometimes haphazard) due diligence to invest in the entrepreneurial opportunities of other entrepreneurs. In 2005, 2.8 percent of adults surveyed in Europe in the *Global Entrepreneurship Monitor* (GEM) were informal investors (see Table 2)[10]. Ireland at 2.3 percent performed better than the UK, which at 1.5 percent was at the bottom of the table. Compare this to countries like Iceland and Norway, where there are large numbers of informal investors.

What financial return do informal investors expect? The median expected payback time is two years and the median amount returned is one times the original investment (see Table 3).. In other words, they expect *zero return on investment*. Interestingly, the payback time and multiple on return are the same for all types of investees except strangers. What's more, the amount invested by strangers is the highest. The most likely reason is that investments by strangers are made in a more detached and business-like manner than investments by relatives and friends.

Table 2 Informal investing in Europe, 2005

Country	Prevalence of informal investors, % of adults 18-64	Average annual investment per investor (2002-2005) (€)
Iceland	6.50	22,246
Norway	5.53	6,008
France	3.85	19,969
Finland	3.46	4,361
Belgium	3.11	20,619
Spain	2.60	6,715
Denmark	2.38	21,003
Ireland	2.31	17,467
Germany	2.12	10,902
Sweden	2.03	12,988
Italy	2.01	8,535
Netherlands	1.81	38,593
Austria	1.79	15,122
UK	1.61	13,921

What kind of people are these informal investors? First and foremost they are: close family relatives of the entrepreneurs (49.4 percent); friends and neighbours (26.4 percent); other relatives (9.4 percent), work colleagues (7.9 percent), and strangers (6.9 percent) as shown in Table 3.

Table 3 Informal Investor and their return expectations

Relationship between Investor-Entrepreneur	Percent total (%)	Mean amount invested (US$)	Median payback time in years (yrs)	Median multiple on return
Close family	49.4	23,190	2	1 X
Other relative	9.4	12,345	2	1 X
Work colleague	7.9	39,032	2	1 X
Friend, neighbour	26.4	15,548	2	1 X
Stranger	6.9	67,672	2-5	1 X
Average		24,202	2	1 X

Look at it this way. Many start-up entrepreneurs mistakenly think they should go straight for venture capital. The truth is that by far the most rare source of capital for new entrepreneurs is venture capital. In Ireland, only 70 companies were backed by VC in 2004.[11] From these data, one could say that the attention paid to venture capital funding is inversely proportional to its importance to start-up entrepreneurs!

Informal investors, on the other hand, spread their money all over the entrepreneurial landscape. In general, classic venture capital flows only to companies with super-star potential, while informal investment flows to companies in all segments including the super-stars. Furthermore, whereas essentially every company begins with informal investment from the 4Fs, very few companies have formal venture capital at the outset. The paradox is that if there were no informal investment, there would be virtually no new ventures. In contrast, if there were no venture capital, millions of new ventures would still be getting off the ground!

Informal investors are on the increase in Northern Ireland. We generally refer to them as providers of "love money". While overall entrepreneurial activity in Northern Ireland is amongst the lowest in the UK[12], this is caused by a combination of factors in the micro and macro-environment, not the least of which are the historical views and traditional perceptions that have hemmed creative thinking. Yet, the rate of business growth in Northern Ireland has increased steadily with the result that entrepreneurial ventures are now in a better position to attract would-be investors. In fact, whilst figures for new start-up ventures in Northern Ireland are lowest amongst the UK regions, survival rate is highest. It is likely that informal investors will provide high support for the minority in the entrepreneurial population – female entrepreneurs and high earners. While the Republic of Ireland has a higher entrepreneurial activity index than Northern Ireland, informal investors have played a key role in supporting nascent entrepreneurs.

Attracting informal investors

How do you attract informal investors? You may have heard of the "elevator pitch" for raising money from venture capital investors. But have you heard of the "kitchen table pitch"? If you are thinking of raising money from someone close to you, here are some tips:

Know your investor's motivations – Some relatives and friends are truly into it for the altruism, but like all people your relatives and friends are also into it for the profit motive. When you are making the pitch around the kitchen table, be sure you list "what is in it for you".

Debt is better than equity for relatives and friends – Equity is "funny money" to most people unless you intend to sell-on the business quickly. Let's say your sister invests €10,000 in your restaurant. The restaurant grows and her equity share grows too. But then you divorce or move and the restaurant simply closes rather than being sold. Make it clear to your sister that she should only give amounts she can afford to lose. Discuss several "what if" scenarios. For instance, what if you go bust or if you relocate or if you hire staff?

Make the pitch in person but follow-up with a written memo – Your relatives don't necessarily care about a formal business plan. But give them some documentation so there's no misunderstanding.[13]

Try to treat them as if they were strangers – Get some distance from the transaction. Have a friend present or have a lawyer prepare the promissory note.

Try to avoid a repayment schedule – Tie your repayments to your cash flow. Give your relative a percentage of your operating cash flow until you have repaid the whole amount. If nothing else, this gives you a constant reminder of your obligation and is less likely to sour your personal relationships.

Don't give voting stock – Often a family member or friend will be willing to finance your start-up but insists on having a voting board seat. One thing you don't want to have is your relative looking over your shoulder and second-guessing every decision.[14]

How to find informal investors

Of course the very best place to find informal investors is your own acquaintance circles. But investor networks are just now starting to flourish around Ireland and the UK. These groups are seeking small start-up businesses worthy of financial support. From informal breakfast groups to broker-forged entities, these networks fill a need among start-ups that have exhausted their personal financial resources – family, friends, and credit cards – but don't yet qualify for venture capital funds. There are number of angel networks and business clusters that can be found through targeting government sources (e.g. Mentor Network Service) or privately managed networks such as First Tuesday, Wireless Wednesday and First Biotech that are operated through Investnet Ltd. These networks can be found on an all-island basis and government-sponsored basis. Business plans for instance can be submitted within a secure environment for investor interest. Here's the short list for early stage finance:

Aspire Micro Loans

Tel: +44 (0) 28 9024 6245
Email: mail@aspire-loans.com
Web: www.aspire-loans.com

Aspire Micro Loans provides finance to businesses established for at least 6 months as sole traders or in partnership. The business can be trading full-time or part-time and employ up to nine members of staff. Aspire Micro Loans aim to grow micro-businesses by providing an account manager, who understands the highs and lows of being in business. They lend small amounts to allow customers to become familiar with using credit and paying it back. Over 90 percent of applications completed are successful. Aspire has invested £800,000 in micro-entrepreneurs in Belfast, a city with a population of only 300,000. Almost 80 percent of loans have gone to the most deprived and under-invested communities (in government-defined "New Targeting Social Need Areas").

First Step

Tel: +353 (1) 260 0988
Email: info@firststep.ie
Web: www.first-step.ie

First Step established in 1991 as a non-profit organisation provides micro-finance, loans of less than €25K to those who are too small to go through the normal channels. In the Year 2000, First Step won a pan-European competition entitled "Access to Finance" for best practice within the Microfinance Industry (MFI). First Step has assisted 1,500 projects and created in excess of 3,000 employment opportunities. First Step is the only MFI operating in Ireland on a nationwide basis also providing mentoring and ongoing support to help micro-scale start-ups. First Step partners include EU Seed and VC Fund, Bank of Ireland, AIB Bank, Enterprise Ireland, European Investment Fund and Department of Social and Family affairs.

National Endowment for Science Technology & the Arts

Tel: +44 (0) 20 7645 9538
Email: nesta@nesta.org.uk
Web: www.nesta.org

NESTA invests in the early stages. NESTA is geared to funding innovation through a range of pioneering and highly diverse programmes for potential entrepreneurs with groundbreaking ideas – from music to microbiology, performance art to artificial intelligence. Whilst NESTA is also funded by an endowment from the National Lottery, there are a number of private investors for business ideas in the mainstream sectors.

Outside investors whose personal investment in a business qualifies under the Enterprise Investment Scheme (Northern Ireland) can enjoy special taxation treatment. There are additional schemes that encourage private investors. For instance, the European Commission approved the Business Expansion and Seed Capital Schemes announced in the Budget 2004 until 2006. The Business Expansion Scheme (BES) allows individuals to invest in businesses for a minimum period of 5 years. The tax paid on any money invested in the scheme is refunded to the investor by the government at the beginning of the scheme, which often means that investors get 42 percent return on investment at the beginning of the investment term. At the end of the 5 years, investors stand to recoup their initial investment as well as getting a return on their investment.

Investments could be made in companies involved in manufacturing, services, tourism, and research and development sectors. Under the Seed Capital Scheme (SCS), individuals who are starting a business get a rebate on taxes they paid in previous years. The size of the rebate depends on the amount of the individual's investment and their effective tax rate. The European Commission has imposed a few limitations on the operation of the schemes. Only small and medium-sized enterprises (SMEs), as defined under EU regulations, may take part in the BES scheme. To qualify as an SME, a company must have turnover of less than €40M in 2004 and less than €50M in 2005. The company may not raise more than €750,000 in any one funding round and may not raise more than €1M over the lifetime of the scheme. Shipbuilding and coal mining enterprises are specifically excluded from the BES and SCS, as are companies that are in difficulties, as defined by the EU guidelines e.g. Sugar beet.

And don't forget to talk to your lawyers and accountants, who are always on the look out for good investments for their clients!

Where to find government financing

Government funding is readily available, but some entrepreneurs think the compliance costs are too high. Ask your friends and acquaintances for recommendations and experiences in applying for and spending government money.

Invest Northern Ireland

Tel: +44 (0) 28 9023 9090

Email: info@investni.com

Web: www.investni.com

Invest Northern Ireland (Invest NI) was established in 2002 under the Industrial Development Act (Northern Ireland) and acts as an umbrella organisation combining the organisation formerly known as the small business agency (LEDU), the local Enterprise Development Unit, the Industrial Development Board (IDB), and the local enterprise agencies as well as other support agencies such as the Industrial Research and Technology Unit (IRTU). As Northern Ireland's now principal economic development agency Invest NI aims to make Northern Ireland an exemplar location for starting and growing a successful business. Invest NI have four main objectives:

Promote innovation in all its aspects – stimulate higher levels of R&D and design and improve knowledge transfer

Achieve higher levels of growth – by indigenous and externally-owned businesses

Promote a more enterprising culture through capability building – so as to raise the overall level of business starts

Attract high quality knowledge based investment from outside Northern Ireland.

Invest NI provides extensive material and expertise on key areas such as turning an idea into a business, buying a franchise, writing a business plan, finance, business tools, marketing, premises, purchasing, staffing and legal issues. It works closely with local District Councils and forms many local partnerships. For instance, it has formed a partnership with Enterprise Northern Ireland to deliver the Northern Ireland Business Start Programme (NIBSP) across Northern Ireland and through local enterprise agencies. For more information on this free programme, visit: www.nibsp.com and to identify the local enterprise agencies you can visit: www.enterpriseni.com/map.htm. Invest NI and the local District Councils provide funding to regional enterprise agencies currently known as Local Enterprise Agencies (LEAs). Note that LEAs focus on supports for pre-start-up, start-up and early development stage businesses in their local area. They provide a range of support services to would-be entrepreneurs and existing small businesses including: advice; mentoring; start your own business training; and grants for start-up and employment.

One particular policy response worth mentioning here is Invest NI's Accelerating Entrepreneurship Strategy (2003-2006). The vision of this strategy is to develop an infrastructure that enables new business ventures to progress and grow rapidly, particularly globally trading and knowledge based projects. It aims to segment businesses into three categories based on the markets in which they will operate and the value added to the Northern Ireland economy. The segments are: Global Markets, External Markets and Local Markets. The transition between market segments should be seamless due to the integrative nature of support from partnerships involving public, private and voluntary sectors. The outcomes of the Accelerating Entrepreneurship Strategy will be measured in terms of entrepreneurial activity and increased volume and value of new business ventures in the Northern Ireland economy.

Enterprise Northern Ireland

Tel: +44 (0) 28 7776 3555

Email: pa@enterpriseni.com

Web: www. enterpriseni.com

Enterprise Northern Ireland is closely linked to Invest NI and focuses on entrepreneurship, business start and business development across all sectors. Enterprise NI is the network of local enterprise agencies in Northern Ireland was established in March 2000. Enterprise Northern Ireland has the following objectives:

To ensure that Enterprise Northern Ireland is a cohesive organisation with members committed to achieving the organisation's vision

To deliver a high quality service to members, sponsors and programme beneficiaries through ongoing evaluation, monitoring and continuous improvement

To secure the long-term sustainability of the service provided at local level through understanding the needs of small businesses, influencing policy, positioning and communication.

Enterprise Northern Ireland is a Northern Ireland-wide organisation with a highly qualified team of experienced business advisors and excellent business facilities. Local Enterprise Agencies are independent not-for-profit companies focusing on local economic and business development led by over 330 voluntary directors, employing almost 200 staff, operating from 42 locations, providing approximately 2,000 businesses units (2 million square feet) and a broad range of training and development. A range of facilities have been developed ideally suited: to hosting training courses and seminars; providing client interview rooms for business advisory/mentoring sessions; and having other support facilities, including secretarial suites, business libraries and ICT facilities. Enterprise NI operates a Small Business Loan Fund that can be accessed through your local enterprise agency. In June 2003, the Board established a Finance and Audit Committee to ensure that systems and processes are subject to continuous review and improvement.

Enterprise Ireland

Tel: +353 (0) 1 808 2000

Email: info@enterpriseireland.ie

Web: www.enterprise-ireland.com

In the south of Ireland, the Culliton Policy Review Group conducted a major policy review in 1991 resulting in the Culliton Report 1992 that made recommendations for better integration of State supports and recommendations for significant change in the regulatory environment where Irish firms would conduct business. A special Task Force on Small Business was appointed to advise government on how best to implement the recommendations of the Culliton Report. The former State agency for indigenous enterprise development (Forbairt), the Trade Board (An Bord Tráchtála) and the industrial training division of the State training and employment authority (Foras Áiseanna Saothair, FAS) were combined under Enterprise Ireland.

Enterprise Ireland was established in 1998 as the Ireland's State agency for enterprise development. Its mission is to accelerate Ireland's development both nationally and in a regional context. Enterprise Ireland works with Irish companies to assist in creating profitable new businesses, build share in international markets, harness new technologies, deepen Research and Development (R&D) capability and build people skills. They offer particular supports in development grants, equity, consulting, training and specialist assistance to existing growth businesses or new businesses employing more than 10 people in the manufacturing and internationally traded services sector. Enterprise Ireland is one of the All-island Student Awards sponsors and introduces entrepreneurship into the schools curriculum.

Allied to Enterprise Ireland

There are additional support agencies that compliment the work of Enterprise Ireland.

City and County Enterprise Boards (CEBs)

Tel: +353 (0) 1 631 2824
Email: info@entemp.ie
Web: www.entemp.ie

Perhaps those rurally located are worth mentioning here. There are various EU programmes that are operated through LEADER companies and funds specific to Irish speaking regions are operated under Údarás na Gaeltachta. City and County Enterprise Boards (CEBs) were formed in each county and/or city of Ireland during 1993/1994 and are different to Enterprise Ireland in that they specialise on supports to develop micro or small indigenous businesses employing less than 10 employees. Typically these businesses would be in the manufacturing and internationally traded services sectors. The Boards provide grants for feasibility studies, capital purchases and employment of staff, start your own business training courses, business development training courses, and mentoring. The National Development plan (NDP) 2000-2006 set down a more varied programme of micro-enterprise supports. These would be delivered by the CEBs under the sub measure One: Selective Financial Intervention Programme which is comprised of grants available to promoters. The grants below, currently under review, are used in the start-up, development and expansion of a micro-enterprise:

A capital grant up to a maximum of 50 percent of the cost of capital and other investment or €75,000 whichever is the lesser

An employment grant of up to €7,500 may be provided in respect of each new full-time job created subject to a limit of 10 jobs

A feasibility study grant where a maximum of 60 percent in the BMW Region or 50 percent in the S&E Region, of the cost of preparing a feasibility study and business plan may be provided subject to a limit of €6,350 in the BMW region, and €5,100 in the S&E region.

For the full CEB listings by city and county, contact the Department of Enterprise, Trade and Employment.

InterTrade Ireland

Tel: +44 (0) 28 3083 4100
Email: info@intertradeireland.com
Web: www.intertradeireland.com

InterTrade Ireland was established as one of the North/South implementation bodies under the British-Irish Agreement Act (1999). The Agreement defines their role as 'A Body to exchange information and co-ordinate work on trade, business development and related matters, in areas where the two administrations specifically agree it would be in their mutual interest. InterTrade Ireland's vision is one of a globally competitive all-island economy characterised by the optimal utilisation of the island's resources, and particularly knowledge resources, to drive competitiveness, growth and wealth creation across this island. InterTrade Ireland aims to lead development of the island economy through distinctive knowledge-based interventions, which will produce significant returns in the areas of cross-border trade, and business development. InterTrade Ireland's seeks to:

- Establishing a channel for North/South trade and business development
- Encouraging the flow and exchange of private equity and venture capital within the two economies of Ireland and between companies and educational establishments
- Supporting business by making recommendations to increase enterprise competitiveness in a North/South context

InterTrade Ireland's value proposition is straightforward: The provision of business solutions that enhance company competitiveness through collaborative all-island initiatives in the following five areas.

- Science, technology and innovation
- Sales & marketing
- Business capability improvement
- Business network support services
- Economic & business research

InterTrade Ireland's Corporate Plan 2005-2007 is now available for download at their website.

InterTrade Ireland's Equity Network

Tel: +44 (0) 28 3083 4151
Email: equity@intertradeireland.com
Web: www.intertradeireland.com

Across the island of Ireland, EquityNetwork is a major initiative of InterTrade Ireland. EquityNetwork plays a key role in assisting businesses in becoming 'investor ready' and providing signposting for equity financing. EquityNetwork compliments the business angel network in Northern Ireland called HALO and provides an is-land-wide education programme to raise awareness of the benefits of using private equity. For instance, it supports a financially substantial (€230,000 in 2004/05) all-island Seedcorn Competition for the best business plans on an annual basis as a direct response to the continuing gap for early stage/start-up funding on the island.

Additional government funding sources

The government listings above are the principal governing bodies for Enterprise across the island of Ireland. Below are a number of additional sources of government assistance. Table 4 helps sort them by function and service rendered.

Table 4 Where to find government assistance

Requirements of assistance	Where to source
Grants for prototype development, feasibility studies or expert advice	Business Link, Department of Trade and Industry, Industrial Development Authority.
Business planning	Investment Belfast, Shell LiveWIRE
Business mentoring	Business in the Community, Northern Ireland Chamber of Commerce and Industry
Investment raising (see previous section)	Department of Enterprise, Trade and Investment, Dublin Business Incubation Centre, Eircom Enterprise Fund, Prince's Trust Northern Ireland
Grants for prototype development, feasibility studies or expert advice	Business Innovation Link, Department of Agriculture and Rural Development, Department of Enterprise, Trade, and Employment, Rural Development Council
Research and Development (R&D) to expand product range	Emergent Business Trust, Ulster Bank (See also technology-specific sources of funding)

Business Link

Tel: +44 (0) 845 600 9006

Email: info@businesslink.gov.uk (Local links also provided)

Web: www. businesslink.gov.uk

Business Link is essentially the government's new small business agency that manages a national network of business link services. These services provide independent and impartial business advice as well as information and a range of services to help small firms and aspiring entrepreneurs. The range of services includes start-up, finance and grants, employing people, exploiting ideas, IT and e-commerce, sales and marketing and growing your business.

Business Innovation Link (BIL)

Tel: +44 (0) 28 9042 7177
Email: info@bus-innovationlink.com
Web: www. bus-innovationlink.com

Business Innovation Link (BIL) focuses on specific support strategies for inventors or innovators. BIL is specifically intended for individuals requiring technical advice and financial support for the design and development of a new product idea with market potential.

The services provided by BIL include financial assistance through grants to progress an idea, IP guidance, technical advice, design and support for prototype manufacturing, feasibility studies, guidance on exploitation with online Kompass searches and mentoring if necessary. Applications to the BIL Award are made through local Invest NI offices.

Business in the Community (BiTC)

Tel: +44 (0) 870 600 2482
Email: information@bitc.org.uk
Web: www.bitc.org.uk

Business in the Community is a unique movement in the UK of 700 member companies, with a further 1600 participating in programmes and campaigns. BiTC operate through a network of 98 local business-led partnerships, as well as working with 45 global partners. BiTC's purpose is to inspire, challenge, engage and support business in continually improving its positive impact on society. They are the largest and longest-established organisation of its kind – an independent business-led charity with over 20 year's experience. Business in the Community has 400 employees across ten regions (48 offices) in the UK, with headquarters in Hackney, London. More than 220 companies are in membership of Business in the Community Northern Ireland which makes an impact across four theme areas: environment, workplace, social impact and economic impact. Members have contributed to the development of BiTC's new strategic plan, which outlines objectives and targets for the next three years. Companies join Business in the Community because they recognise the value of integrating policy and practice and the internal dialogue this prompts.

Department of Agriculture and Rural Development

Tel: +44 (0) 28 9052 4999
Email: dardhelpline@dardni.gov.uk
Web: www. dardni.gov.uk

The mission statement of the Department of Agriculture and Rural Development is "To promote economic growth and the development of the countryside in Northern Ireland. It will assist the competitive development of the agri-food, fishing and forestry sectors of the NI economy, being responsive to the needs of consumers for safe and wholesome food, the welfare of animals and the conservation of the environment". The Department of Agriculture and Rural Development has a knowledge base index for different business areas and offers a number of financial-assistance schemes. They provide a range of services to help develop a business idea and assist with business training and planning both in local and international markets. One example is the training and expertise given to rural diversification projects from Rural Connect Advisors, more information can be found by visiting: http://www.ruralni.gov.uk

The Department also has a dedicated food business incubation centre at CAFRE, Loughry Campus, the only one of its kind on the island of Ireland. In the south of Ireland there area also a number of agri-specific bodies such as Teagasc, the Irish Agriculture and Development Authority visit: www.teagasc.ie; Bord Bia, the Irish Food Board visit www.bordbia.ie and Coillte, the Irish Forestry Company visit: www. Coillte.ie as well as a number of development centres including Food Product Development Centre or Tourism Research Centre based at Dublin Institute of Technology.

Department of Enterprise, Trade and Employment

Tel: +353 (0) 1 631 2824

Email: info@entemp.ie

Web: www.entemp.ie

The Department of Enterprise, Trade and Employment is structured into seven functional divisions, but there is also a substantial degree of co-operation and inter-action between units. There are over 1,000 staff employed in the Department in offices abroad in London, Brussels and Geneva and throughout the country – one office in Kilkenny, different locations in Dublin and a new office in Carlow as a result of decentralising. The Department seeks to equitably grow Ireland's competitiveness and quality employment under four action points:

- Enterprise, innovation, growth
- Quality work and learning
- Making markets and regulation work better
- Business delivery, modernisation and customer focus

Note that there was a fifth pillar in 2003-2005 Strategy, the European Union, which is no longer a benchmark since the Irish economy is growing at more than twice the EU average. A new Statement of Strategy, covering the period 2005-2007 builds upon the Enterprise Strategy Group report *Ahead of the Curve* and outlines the need for Ireland to know how to deal with emergent competitive threats. In order to contribute towards the Lisbon goal to make Europe the most competitive knowledge-based economy in the world and compete with the US, the Irish economy might be in a position to finance emerging e-commerce in Ireland. There are organisations providing assistance specific to the needs of e-businesses, including Empower.ie (visit: www.empower.ie) and those simply providing an electronic tool to deliver targeted information and trading opportunities to companies throughout Ireland such as TradeNetIreland (visit: www.tradenetireland.com).

Within the island the 2003-2005 Strategy aims to further unlock the potential for North/South trade – 2003 statistics show that Northern Ireland exported €1.04 billion worth of manufacturing goods to the South, and the south exported €1.41 billion to the North. The Irish Exporters Association can provide useful export information, visit: www.irishexporters.ie. The performance indicators that will be used to evaluate the success of this strategy include firm internationalisation, increase in R&D and rate of entrepreneurship.

The Department also has policy responsibility for a number of state-sponsored bodies some of which have been mentioned above including City and County Enterprise Boards, Competition Authority, FÁS, Forfás (Forfás is the national policy and advisory board for enterprise, trade, science, technology and innovation and delegates power to Enterprise Ireland for indigenous industry and IDA Ireland for inward investment), InterTrade Ireland, Science Foundation Ireland and Shannon Development.

Shannon Development established InnovationsWorks an initiative to create state-of-the-art business incubation centres – to stimulate entrepreneurial potential and to develop a sustainable enterprise culture in the Shannon Region. Each InnovationWorks facility is located within a Shannon Development Knowledge Network location; these include technology parks in counties Limerick, Kerry, Tipperary, Offaly (Birr), and Clare (Ennis). Shannon Development invests in companies that are likely to achieve significant sales growth of €1 million and employ in excess of 10 people within 3 years of start-up.

Department of Enterprise, Trade and Investment

Tel: +44 (0) 28 9052 9900

Email: information@ detini.gov.uk

Web: www.detini.gov.uk

The Department of Enterprise, Trade and Investment (DETI) is responsible for economic policy development, energy, tourism, mineral development, health and safety at work, Companies Registry, Insolvency Service, consumer affairs, and labour market and economic statistics services. It also has a role in ensuring the provision of appropriate infrastructure for a modern economy. Economics, financial and personnel management services are provided centrally within the Department. DETI has four agencies, established as non-departmental public bodies (NDPBs), to assist in strategy implementation, they include:

Invest Northern Ireland (Invest NI)

Northern Ireland Tourist Board (NITB)

Health and Safety Executive for Northern Ireland (HSENI)

General Consumer Council for Northern Ireland (GCCNI).

DETI is responsible for developing and implementing the 3 programmes under the EU Structural Funds, which complement the Departments strategy and its wider objectives. The programmes are the EU Programme for Peace and Reconciliation in Northern Ireland and the Border Counties of Ireland 2000-2004 (PEACE II), INTERREG IIIA Ireland/Northern Ireland Programme 2000-06, and Measure 4

(Local Economic Development) under Priority 1 (Economic Growth and Competitiveness) of the Northern Ireland Building Sustainable Prosperity Programme.

The purpose of the Departmental Board is to manage Departmental business at a strategic level and to make strategic decisions in relation to economic development policies, strategies of and allocation of resources to DETI agencies, corporate and operating plans.

Department of Trade and Industry

Tel: +44 (0) 20 7215 5000

Email: dti.enquiries@dti.gsi.gov.uk

Web: www.dti.gov.uk

The Department of Trade and Industry (DTI) has the driving ambition of "prosperity for all" by working to create the best environment for business success in the UK and fair and open markets in the UK, Europe and the world. DTI's vision is to drive up sustainable economic growth under three strategic objectives: supporting successful business, promoting science and innovation and ensuring fair markets.

DTI helps people and companies become more productive by promoting enterprise, innovation and creativity. They champion UK business at home and abroad (through UK Trade and Investment with the Foreign and commonwealth Office) and invest heavily in world-class science and technology. For example DTI have published a Manufacturing Strategy and launched the Manufacturing Advisory Service, which has helped over 2,200 companies to increase their added value by an average of £106,000 and has provided an actual total value added to UK manufacturers approaching £86 million. DTI published *The Innovation Report* (December 2003) identifying areas of relative UK underperformance and sets out clear proposals and an action plan to achieve the Prime Minister's vision of the UK as a key knowledge hub in the global economy.

DTI leads the Office of Science and Technology (OST). During 2005/06 financial year, the OST invested £3 billion in UK research which will rise to £3.4 billion by 2007/08. DTI also invests in knowledge transfer through the £187 million Higher Education Innovation Fund (HEIF) to support the exchange of people and ideas between the research base and users, including the "spin out" and licensing activities of universities and public sector research establishments.

Dublin Business Innovation Centre

Tel: +353 (0) 1 671 3111

Email: dsscf@dbic.ie

Web: www.dbic.ie

Dublin Business Innovation Centre manages the Dublin Seed Capital Fund and Irish BICs Seed Capital Fund. The Centre was established in 1987 with private, public, educational and EU support. It provides advice to new business projects and access to seed and early-stage equity capital to emerging, start-up and developing companies across a range of technology-led sectors, Telecoms, software and other sectors. Dublin BIC particularly plays a facilitator role to the entrepreneur in finding practical solutions to problems in a responsive non-bureaucratic way. These activities complement the assistance and services provided by the State agencies, EU Programmes and the private sector. Dublin BIC can help improve business survival rates by providing selective assistance and support through the first 3-5 years by offering business development planning through its after-care services.

Eircom Enterprise Fund

Tel: +353 (0) 1 647 1866

Email: mmoore@eircom.ie

Web: www.eircom-enterprise-fund.ie

The Eircom Enterprise Fund incorporated in 1998 is a joint venture between telecoms incumbent Eircom and Enterprise Ireland. It provides risk capital to young high growth companies operating in the technology, media and telecoms (TMT) sector. The €2.54 million fund is now committed.

Emerging Business Trust

Tel: +44 (0) 28 9031 1660

Email: info@emergingbusinesstrust.com

Web: www.emergingbusinesstrust.com

What is interesting about the Emerging Business Trust fund is that it supports niche businesses with an emphasis on technology. This area represents 30 percent of the portfolio. The Emerging Business Trust (EBT) is funded through Invest NI and International Fund of Ireland (IFI). The body IFI was set up in 1987 following the Anglo-Irish Agreement, to assist in the development of Northern Ireland and its Border Counties. IFI has targeted business enterprise as one of its key objectives and to this end it set up a Pilot Loan Scheme for businesses in disadvantaged area of Northern Ireland. EBT took over the successful pilot scheme in October 1996. The Scheme proceeded to exceed all expectations in terms of demand and quality of all businesses supported. EBT is a successful loan fund targeting high value start-ups or expanding businesses. EBT has assisted 241 businesses and helped to leverage a total of £27 million. Typically, client companies employ in the region of 10-15 employees but the objective is to make contributions even larger and more innovative.

Investment Belfast

Tel: +44 (0) 28 9033 1136

Email: info@investmentbelfast.com

Web: www. investmentbelfast.com

Investment Belfast provides a gateway service that entails providing key business information and researches including area profile and sector analysis – sectors include retail, leisure, ICT, life sciences and biotechnology and the creative industries. It organises fact-finding visits to meet civic and business leaders and key agencies. They also have a key role in facilitating introductions between nascent entrepreneurs and financiers, business support agencies and business leaders as well as conducting property searches.

In the educational context, Investment Belfast supports the annual £25K Award for New Entrepreneurs, a business plan competition open to partner institutions of the Northern Ireland Centre for Entrepreneurship (NICENT). They are involved in expanding the clinical research base by undertaking trials in Northern Ireland and marketing this capability to the pharmaceutical industry. They have a cluster that is currently engaging in clinical services with a range of global clients, from multinational pharmaceutical to start-up biotech companies and academic institutions. They also have an innovative scheme designed to benefit up-and-coming entrepreneurs through incubation and mentoring processes.

Industrial Development Authority (IDA)

Tel: +353 (0) 1 603 4000
Email: idaireland@ida.ie
Web: www.idaireland.com

The Industrial Development Authority is the primary government agency responsible for attracting foreign direct investment to Ireland as well as developing the portfolio of overseas business. It provides a full range of assistance both financial and advisory, to attract and support foreign direct investment. IDA focus on business sectors that are closely matched with the emerging needs of the economy and that can operate competitively in global markets from an Irish base. They build links between international businesses and third level education and research centres to ensure the necessary skills and research and capabilities are in place and build world-leading clusters of knowledge-based activities. IDA have a strong influence on the competitive needs of the economy. Hence they are actively involved in developing infrastructure and business support services, telecoms, education, regulatory issues especially in relation to EU policy. In 2003 IDA negotiated and secured 64 inward investment projects and IDA supported companies spent €14.7 billion in the Irish economy from their annual sales of €69.3 billion and exports of €65.2 billion.

Northern Ireland Chamber of Commerce and Industry

Tel: +44 (0) 28 9024 4113
Email: mail@northernirelandchamber.com
Web: www.nicci.co.uk

The Northern Ireland Chamber of Commerce and Industry is Northern Ireland's largest, independent business body accessing to more than 4,000 member businesses representing every sector of the business community, from the sole trader to businesses with thousands of employees. It is also the largest private-sector forum in Northern Ireland. Its mission is to:

Continue to grow and develop its membership

Develop a range of membership services and ensure that these remain relevant to the needs of its members

Represent, vigorously and practically, the interests of its members to all appropriate influencers and to play a key role in improving the business performance of its members in their home and export markets

Every quarter the Chamber in association with BT carries out Northern Ireland's biggest business confidence survey (n=2,000) across all sectors of the local economy. Since entrepreneurs analyse their own prospects for growth and employment and the climate affecting business confidence, the survey is an important barometer and has become one of the most reliable yardsticks not only of Northern Ireland's SME sector but also its economic health.

Prince's Trust Northern Ireland

Tel: +44 (0) 28 9074 5454

Email: ptnire@princes-trust.org.uk

Web: www.princes-trust.org.uk

The Prince's Trust is a UK wide initiative established by the Prince of Wales. The Charity provides practical support including training, mentoring and financial assistance for 14-30 year olds who need assistance in realising their potential and transforming their lives. Grants are provided for jobs, training and group projects. 12,793 young entrepreneurs went through the Prince's Trust Business Start Programme last year. This programme offers a low interest loan of up to £4,000 for a sole trader, or up to £5,000 for a partnership (the average loan is between £2,000 and £3,000 but varies regionally). A test-marketing grant of up to £250 is also provided as well as ongoing business support and specialist advice such as the free Legal Helpline and ongoing advice from a volunteer business mentor and free or discounted access to a wide range of products and services.

Rural Development Council

Tel: +44 (0) 28 8676 6980

Email: info@rdc.org.uk

Web: www.rdc.org.uk

The Rural Development Council was established to address the needs of deprived rural areas in Northern Ireland. Its vision is: "A rural Northern Ireland which makes a full and balanced contribution to the development of the region". Therefore its central objective is to influence policy and deliver practical programmes. Two of its key principals are to encourage economic innovation and to build effective partnerships. The Council operates a range of grant assistance schemes, the most commonly known is the development and management of the PEACE II programme. The Policy and Innovation Research Unit is based at the RDC and launched Northern Ireland's first rural baseline project in September 2001 marking a key milestone in the efforts of the RDC to establish a set of indicators that might assist in the achievement of sustainable rural development in Northern Ireland. The first report entitled *A Picture of Rural Change 2002* presents and interprets data from a wide and varied range of sources.

Shell LiveWIRE

Tel: +44 (0) 28 9045 4510

Email: shell-livewire@pne.org

Web: www. shell-livewire.org

Shell LiveWIRE provides information, advice and practical support for 16-30 year olds with business ideas and the desire to start up their own business. They offer expertise in key areas of general management, sales and marketing, business planning, finance and personnel. They are actively involved in enterprise shows and providing business toolkits specific to business ideas and an interactive web service for the exchange of ideas. For example they have a finance action planner, which helps you to start your own finance action plan. In conjunction with Invest NI, services for young entrepreneurs are available with a number of live case studies. ShellLive WIRE also hosts a high profile competition for young entrepreneurs involved in new business start-ups in Northern Ireland, one winner from the 10 finalists proceeds from the regional event to the UK final.

Ulster Bank

Tel: +44 (0) 28 9024 4112

Email: businessbanking@ulsterbank.com

Web: www. ulsterbank.com

Ulster Bank is highly committed to creating new and growing small businesses as it employs dedicated commercial managers and provides a comprehensive 'Start-up in Business' guide plus an attractive financial package. For instance, its Small Loans Guarantee Scheme that is supported by government recognises the important contribution of small businesses to the Northern Ireland economy by providing up to 75 percent loan for businesses without a track record or the necessary security. Ulster Bank have also teamed up with Invest NI and Enterprise Ireland to sponsor the All-island Student Enterprise Awards, a business plan competition similar to £25K but open to all students in third level education institutes on the island.

Since over 80 percent of capital raised in Ireland according to the Irish Venture Capital Association (IVCA) is for investment in high technology companies, it is important to outline the differences between investment preferences for entrepreneurial technologists across the island working within universities or in industry. There is one initiative FUSION that is the first all-island network between industry and academia. FUSION enables knowledge and technology transfer across the island, supporting business innovation and increased capability. FUSION achieves this by establishing and supporting three-way cross-border partnerships between companies with technology based development needs, research centres with specialist expertise and high calibre graduates. To date FUSION has enabled over 65 companies to innovate and improve their competitiveness by applying R&D excellence which was previously unavailable to them. The new round of funding will extend those opportunities to a further 130 companies until at least 2007.

Academic and industry sources

The list below contains a mixture of investment sources from academia and industry.

4th Level Ventures/University Seed Fund Ltd Partnership

Tel: +353 (0) 1 671 1288
Email: dennis.jennings@4thLevelVentures.ie
Web: www. 4thLevelVentures.ie

4th Level Ventures is a €20 million Venture Capital Fund. Investors will invest in high potential businesses in the seed or early stages of their development. The difference is that the fund was established to commercialise the business opportunities i.e. technology and IP, that arise from research in Irish third level educational institutes including Institutes of Technology and Universities. They are neutral and often work on campus with University innovation or commercialisation teams. Although one of the more recently established funds (Est. 2002) their portfolio is impressive including pharmaceutical/Agrochemical companies such as Celtic Catalysts Ltd. and software businesses including PixAlert Limited.

NITECH Growth Fund

Tel: +44 (0) 28 9024 4424
Email: nitechgrowthfund@ANGLETechnology.com
Web: www.nitechgrowthfund.co.uk

The NITECH Growth Fund was established by Invest NI providing early stage funding to take an R&D Project to proof of concept and commercialisation. The fund provides staged investments ranging from £20,000-200,000 with a maximum total investment of £250,000 being provided to any one company. The fund complements existing public sector grants and other venture capital funds active in providing early-stage funding and is managed by ANGLE Technology Limited, in conjunction with Clarendon Fund Managers Limited. NITECH is open not only to individual researchers, research teams and university departments but also existing small and medium-sized companies.

QUBIS LTD

Tel: +44 (0) 28 9068 2321
Email: info@qubis.co.uk
Web: www.qubis.co.uk

QUBIS LTD focuses on investment for early stage technology companies and on commercialising the University's research and development activities through the formation of 'spin out' businesses. It was established by Queens University in 1984 and has a portfolio of 34 technology companies based in Northern Ireland. In 2004, the combined turnover was £47 million employing 718 people with 95 percent of sales being internationally exported. QUBIS LTD takes an equity holding in a new spin out venture in return for an investment of cash and/or IP. While QUBIS LTD is enthusiastic about investing in at least 1 to 2 new ventures per annum, as a holding company they are patient investors. Some of the companies on its portfolio include USA-based Andor, Amacis and Amphion.

Seroba BioVentures/Irish Bioscience Venture Capital Fund

Tel: +353 (0) 1 214 0400

Email: info@seroba.ie

Web: www.seroba.ie

Seroba BioVentures manages the Irish BioSciences Venture Capital Fund (IBVCF), This fund will invest in both seed and early stage projects within the biotechnology, pharmaceutical and medical fields and it is Ireland's first venture capital fund exclusively dedicated to the life science and medical device sectors on the island of Ireland. Generally Seroba BioVentures considers proposals from leading research institutes, universities, research hospitals and from existing companies. The €20 million fund was launched in February 2002 and also invests in inward bound projects emanating from other countries. Note that the European Investment Bank, the European Union's long-term financing institution concluded €50 million agreement with Merlin European Biosciences Fund to provide equity capital for leading European bioscience companies in 1999, for further information visit www.eib.eu.int.

Trinity Venture Fund

Tel: +353 (0) 1 205 7700

Email: info@tvc.com

Web: www.tvc.com

Trinity Venture Capital is part of the Reihill Venture Capital Group. Trinity invests in early stage and expanding Irish technology companies. Established in September 1997, it has €163 million under management in Trinity Fund 1 and €139 million in Trinity Fund 2 and has an investment portfolio which reflects Ireland's strong performance in the technology sector. Trinity Venture Capital typically invests between €1 million and €6 million in an initial investment with up to €15 million available over a number of investment rounds. Where appropriate, larger sums can also be sourced through Trinity's partners. The investors in the Trinity Fund 2 mainly consist of leading Irish and international financial institutions. The Reihill Venture Capital Group currently has over €235 million under management. Trinity typically look to realise investments in 3-7 years but both Trinity Venture Capital and strategic partners always have an eye to the long term.

University Challenge Fund Northern Ireland

Tel: +44 (0) 28 9068 2321
Email: info@qubis.co.uk
Web: www.ucfni.org

The University Challenge Fund of £2.75 million is managed by QUBIS LTD. and was established in 1999 to facilitate the commercialisation of innovative research being carried out within Northern Ireland's two universities, Queen's University Belfast and the University of Ulster. The fund is a result of a successful joint university bid to assist universities in securing the utility of their discoveries. Its broad objective is to make the region more innovative, by increasing the number of high-grade technology based companies. The specific objective of UCF (NI) is to increase the number of good ideas originating from the Northern Ireland universities that are developed to a stage where they are able to attract funding through existing channels. Investment ranges from up to £100,000 in new spin out ventures, which means that both universities can fund larger amounts in the earlier seed stages than is possible through their individual later-stage funds from QUBIS LTD. and UUTECH Ltd. It is therefore anticipated that the seed fund will lead to a significant increase in the number of follow-on deals in which venture capitalists, corporate venturers and business angels decide to invest in NI based high technology firms.

UUTECH

Tel: +44 (0) 28 9093 0008
Email: info@uutech.co.uk
Web: www.uutech.co.uk

UUTech is a Technology and Knowledge Transfer company of the University of Ulster established in 1998 to manage the evaluation and exploitation of the University's IP. More recently, in September 2004, UUTech launched a broader and more commercially driven vision and has stronger collaboration/ consultancy with the industry in particular aspects of life sciences, physical science, humanities and social sciences. Their primary objective is to provide the highest levels of wealth and skills creation and inspire and nurture enterprise and innovation through harvesting new discoveries of university research. They have key strengths in evaluating new technologies for patentability and commercial potential; marketing inventions; identifying and procuring funds for seed capital, expansion and market penetration; and negotiating the sale or licensing of inventions. Its portfolio contains companies such as Causeway Data Communications and Datactics.

Western Development Commission/Western Investment Fund

Tel: +353 (0) 94 986 1441
Email: info@wdc.ie
Web: www.wdc.ie

The WDC is responsible for the management and administration of the €32 million Western Investment Fund (WIF) which provides risk capital by way of equity and loans, on a commercial basis, to projects and businesses in seed, early stage or development stage capital to realise growth potential. WIF offers capital to SMEs based in, or locating to, the Western Region. Investments will typically range from €100,000-1 million (€750,000 in Clare subject to State aid rules). WDC also provides funding for MBOs. Financial returns are revolved and invested in other viable projects within the Western region. The Sectors targeted for investment are Manufacturing and internationally traded services, Information & communications technology, Life Sciences & medical devices, Tourism and Food, fisheries and natural resources.

Note that in the Galetacht areas to the western edge, Donegal, Mayo, Galway and Kerry, and parts counties Cork, Meath and Waterford, an economic development organisation called Údarás Na Gaeltachta is charged with delivering support to individuals, projects, and SMEs in these Irish-speaking regions. Much of the success of the Gaeltacht is in attracting mobile international investment due to the financial and tax incentives on offer in the modern infrastructural setting of Ireland. Sectors for investment include marine, aquaculture, manufacturing and internationally traded services. For more information visit: www.udaras.ie.

To conclude, there are dozens of organisations out there (some often overlooked) that can assist entrepreneurs in getting advice and support in minority areas and emergent sectors. For instance, Women in Technology and Science (WITS) was established in 1990, visit: www.witsireland.com or Creative Ireland is a useful site detailing forums for the arts industry, visit www.creativeireland.com.

Bank or equity financing?

Entrepreneurs need both debt financing and equity financing—all at the right time. Equity financing is best in the early start-up stages, especially during R&D and product development. It is also quite appropriate in later rounds, for example when bringing on highly qualified staff, ramping up sales, for marketing and acceleration purposes. Debt financing is best used for working capital and to build up the infrastructure.

Most entrepreneurs start out by financing growth through equity and then move on to sources of debt funding once they have built up value. Usually debt is cheaper than giving equity away in the early stages of an investment. But equity investors (both passive and active) are willing to take greater risk; hence your potential for reward should be greater.

How do debt and equity ultimately affect profitability or cash flow? Debt financing involves a payback of the funds plus a fee (called interest) for the use of the money. Equity financing involves a transfer of ownership and a payback of dividends for the use of the money. Debt places a burden of repayment and interest on the entrepreneur, while equity financing forces the entrepreneur to relinquish some degree of ownership and control. In the extreme, the choice for the entrepreneur is (1) to take on debt without giving up ownership in the venture or (2) to relinquish a percentage of ownership in order to avoid having to borrow. In most cases, a combination of debt and equity proves most appropriate. The next section and Table 5 below summarise the differences between equity and debt financing.

Debt financing

Many new ventures find that debt financing (you get a loan and repay at a predetermined interest rate) is necessary. Short-term borrowing (one year or less) is often required for working capital and is repaid out of the proceeds from sales or other revenue. Long-term debt (term loans of one to five years or long-term loans maturing in more than five years) is used to finance the purchase of property or equipment, with the purchased asset serving as collateral for the loans. Commercial banks are the major source of debt financing.

Table 5 How finance options will affect profitability or cash flow[15]

Equity Financing		Debt Financing	
Advantages	**Disadvantages**	**Advantages**	Disadvantages
Can provide a large injection of capital	Capital is usually only available in very large amounts	Amount borrowed can vary according to your needs	It creates a debt obligation
No interest payments	It means 'selling' a part of your business	As long as it is repaid, it will not affect your ownership of the company	Interest will be charged – affecting profitability
No obligation to repay capital	Venture capitalists expect high returns on their investments (at least 25 percent per annum)		Collateral is usually required and banks will value your assets conservatively

Dealing with commercial banks

Although some banks will make unsecured short-term loans, e.g. Ulster Bank's Small Loans Guarantee Scheme, most bank loans are secured by fixed assets, receivables (amount owed by customers), inventories, or other assets. In about 90 percent of these cases, banks require collateral, generally consisting of stocks, machinery, equipment, and real estate, and require systematic payments over the life of the loan. Whether in the UK or Ireland, banks are not interested in the entrepreneurs' future prospects and do not really look at business plans indicating the viability of businesses and their capacity to meet debt repayments out of cash flow.

Yet these days entrepreneurs can actually expect more from a bank that just a loan. In the USA, banks offer a number of services to a new venture, including computerized payroll preparation, letters of credit, international services, lease financing, and money market accounts. Look for this trend to expand internationally.

To secure a bank loan, an entrepreneur typically will have to answer a number of questions. Five of the most common questions, together with descriptive commentaries, follow.

What do you plan to do with the money? Do not plan on using funds for a high-risk venture. Banks seek the most secure venture possible.

How much do you need? Some entrepreneurs go to their bank with no clear idea of how much money they need. All they know is that they want money. The more precisely the entrepreneur can answer this question and realistically as opposed to conservatively, the more likely the loan will be granted.

When do you need it? Never rush to the bank with immediate requests for money with no plan. Such a strategy shows that the entrepreneur is a poor planner, and most lenders will not want to get involved.

How long will you need it? The shorter the period of time the entrepreneur needs the money, the more likely he or she is to get the loan. The time at which the loan will be repaid should correspond to some important milestone in the business plan.

How will you repay the loan? This is the most important question. What if plans go awry? Can other income be diverted to pay off the loan? Does collateral exist? Even if a quantity of fixed assets exists, the bank may be unimpressed because it knows from experience that assets sold at a liquidation auction bring only a fraction of their value. Five to ten percent is not unusual.[16]

Remember that banks are businesses too. They have stockholders to whom they must report and they are highly regulated by federal and state agencies. They may sometimes not lend to certain industries based on their corporate policy.

Debt financing has both advantages and disadvantages. On the plus side, you don't have to give up ownership of your company. More borrowing allows for potentially greater return on equity and gives you a challenge to work towards. And during periods of low interest rates, the opportunity cost is justified since the cost of borrowing is low. On the minus side, you'll have regular (monthly) interest payments. Continual cash-flow problems can be intensified because of payback responsibility. And heavy use of debt can inhibit growth and development.

Sources of debt financing

Other debt-financing sources include trade credit, accounts receivable factoring, finance companies, leasing companies, mutual savings banks, savings and loan associations, and insurance companies. Table 6 provides a summary of these sources, the business types they often finance, and their financing terms.

Trade credit is credit given by suppliers who sell goods on account. This credit is reflected on the entrepreneur's balance sheet as accounts payable, and in most cases it must be paid in 30 to 90 days. Many small, new businesses obtain this credit when no other form of financing is available to them. Suppliers typically offer this credit as a way of attracting new customers.

Accounts receivable financing is short-term financing that involves either the pledge of receivables as collateral for a loan or the sale of receivables (factoring). Accounts receivable loans are made by commercial banks, whereas factoring is done primarily by commercial finance companies and factoring concerns.

Accounts receivable bank loans are made on a discounted value of the receivables pledged. A bank may make receivable loans on a notification or non-notification plan. Under the notification plan, purchasers of goods are informed that their accounts have been assigned to the bank. They then make payments directly to the bank, which credits them to the borrower's account. Under the non-notification plan, borrowers collect their accounts as usual and then pay off the bank loan.

Factoring is the sale of a business's accounts receivable. Under this arrangement, the receivables are sold, at a discounted value, to a factoring company. Some commercial finance companies also do factoring. Under a standard arrangement the factor will buy the client's receivables outright, without recourse, as soon as the client creates them by its shipment of goods to customers. Factoring fits some businesses better than others, and it has become almost traditional in industries such as textiles, furniture manufacturing, clothing manufacturing, toys, shoes, and plastics.

Hire purchase is an extended payment scheme entered into between the entrepreneur/hirer and the owner (equipment manufacturer or financial institution). Under the HP, the hirer only needs to pay a small deposit upfront, and then make regular instalment payments. Only upon final instalment does the hirer acquire ownership.

Table 6 Common debt-financing sources

Type	Source	Business type financed		Financing term		
		Start-up firm	Existing firm	Short term	Interme-diate	Long term
Trade credit	Suppliers	Yes	Yes	Yes	No	
Accounts receivable	Commercial banks	No	Yes	Yes	Seldom	No
Factors	Commercial finance com-panies	Seldom	Yes	Most frequent	Seldom	No
Commercial banks		Sometimes, but only if strong capital or collateral exists	Yes	Fre-quently	Some-times	Seldom
Hire pur-chase	Equipment manufacturer or financial institution	Yes, if company has demon-strated sales	Yes	Yes	Yes	Seldom
Finance companies	Asset-based lenders	Sometimes, if company shows business case	Yes	Most frequent	Yes	Seldom
Lending companies	Lenders	Seldom	Yes	No	Most frequent	Occasio nally
Saving / associa-tions	Depositors	Seldom	Real estate only	No	No	Real estate only
Insurance companies	Assets	Rarely	Yes	No	No	Yes

Finance companies are asset-based lenders that lend money against assets such as receivables, inventory, and equipment. The advantage of dealing with a commercial finance company is that it often will make loans that banks will not. The interest rate varies from 2 to 6 percent over that charged by a bank. New ventures that are unable to raise money from banks and factors often turn to finance companies.

Other ways to raise cash include equity instruments (discussed in the next section), which give investors a share of the ownership. Here are some preliminary examples.

Loan with warrants provides the investor with the right to buy stock at a fixed price at some future date. Terms on the warrants are negotiable. The warrant customarily provides for the purchase of additional stock, such as up to 10 percent of the total issue at 130 percent of the original offering price within a five-year period following the offering date.

Convertible debentures are unsecured loans that can be converted into stock. The conversion price, the interest rate, and the provisions of the loan agreement are all areas for negotiation.

Preferred stock is equity that gives investors a preferred place amongst the creditors in the event the venture is dissolved. The stock also pays a dividend and can increase in price, thus giving investors an even greater return. Some preferred stock issues are convertible to common stock, a feature that can make them even more attractive.

Common stock is the most basic form of ownership. This stock usually carries the right to vote for the board of directors. If a new venture does well, common stock investors often make a large return on their investment. These stock issues often are sold through public or private offerings.

Global entrepreneurs today are exposed to all kinds of potential losses. It is often wise to take out political risk insurance for losses resulting from risks associated with cross-border transactions, primarily in developing countries, including confiscation, expropriation, nationalisation, contract frustration, licence cancellation or the non-honouring of guarantees. It protects against physical damage to assets resulting from political violence, including war and civil uprisings. It can protect investments, plant and machinery, inventories, and contracts. Political risk insurance also protects against actions of the entrepreneur's home government, such as embargo and forced cancellation.

Types of equity financing

E quity financing is money invested in the venture with no legal obligation for entrepreneurs to repay the principal amount or pay interest on it. The use of equity funding thus requires no repayment in the form of debt. It does, however, require sharing the ownership and profits with the funding source. Since no repayment is required, equity capital can be much safer for new ventures than debt financing. Yet the entrepreneur must consciously decide to give up part of the ownership in return for this funding.[17]

Equity capital can be raised through two major sources: public stock offerings and private placements. In both cases, entrepreneurs must follow the local laws pertaining to raising such funds. The entire process can be difficult, expensive, and time-consuming. On the other hand, successful stock offerings can help a fledgling enterprise raise a great deal of money. Let's look at public offereings first.

What are public offerings?

One type of equity financing is the Initial Public Offering (IPO). This is a company's first-ever sale of shares to the public. In many cases, it's the first time people outside the company have the opportunity to buy its shares. That's why a company is often said to be going public or floating when it conducts an IPO. Here are some of the advantages to this approach.

- **Size of capital amount** – Selling securities is one of the fastest ways to raise large sums of capital in a short period of time.

- **Liquidity** – The public market provides liquidity for owners since they can readily sell their stock.

- **Value** – The marketplace puts a value on the company's stock, which in turn allows value to be placed on the corporation.

- **Image** – The image of a publicly traded corporation often is stronger in the eyes of suppliers, financiers, and customers.[8]

The global IPO market

The global IPO market has been a rollercoaster. The "crash" of 1998-1999 and the subsequent drop in IPOs still have not seen a full recovery. One of the key global developments of late is the increased numbers of companies dual or even triple tracking – simultaneously preparing themselves for an IPO, a trade sale or venture capital/private equity round, depending on the balance of the advantage.

A survey by Ernst & Young (2004) revealed that 2004 was an important turning point for IPO activity around the world with an increase for the first time since 2000 in both the number of IPOs and the total capital raised. There were 1516 flotations globally in 2004 raising $124 billion of capital with every major region showing an increase in activity. According to the Global IPO Survey 2005, in the UK during 2004, there were 191 IPOs with total capital raised reaching €6,8 billion whilst IPO activity Ireland was much less at 5 IPOs and €1,5 billion total capital raised. Note: this makes the capital raised by Irish IPOs 8 times larger than their UK counterparts, which is likely due to London's junior market, AIM. AIM's advantages are small size, less stringent regulations and accelerated IPO (scale of weeks).[18] The largest UK IPO in 2004 was Premier Foods, raising proceeds of nearly $752 million followed by Halfords Group raising $562 million and Admiral with $477 million. The UK differs though from the rest of Europe with large volumes of modest transactions, whereas countries such as France, Germany Italy and Belgium centred on a small number of relatively substantial transactions, for example the IPO of Belgacom in Belgium raising $4.4 billion.

In Ireland, IPO activity has increased from 2003 when it did more than €1 billion of IPO business. In 2005, IPO activity reached €1.5 billion; this could be due in part to the 35 percent increase in capital investment from the €31.23 million in Q1 2004, to €42.11 million in Q1 2005. The €42.11 million invested in the first quarter of 2005 is also an increase of 97 percent from the last quarter of 2004, when the amount invested was €21.37 million. Ireland had a total of eight deals this quarter, down from ten deals in Q4 2004 and Q1 2004. As throughout 2004, Ireland retains its 7th place in the first quarter of 2005 for number of deals. In terms of amounts raised, Ireland has slipped down to 8th place, mainly due to increased venture capital activity in Denmark.

In 2005, globally the picture is not so clear as Q1 2005 saw a relatively modest 247 IPOs internationally although the capital raised held up at $24 billion, down only slightly from Q1 2004. Uncertainty over oil prices, the new European prospectus directive and the Chinese economy overheating are all cited as possible reasons for the more guarded optimism.

The mechanics of going public

An initial public offering (IPO) can be tough, expensive and complex. With all the accounting, financial reporting and security law, the average entrepreneur usually does not have expertise in these areas. Entrepreneurs should be aware of the concerns confronting them when pursuing the IPO market. Many new ventures recognize some disadvantages of going public. A few of these include:

Costs – The expenses involved with a public offering are significantly higher than for other sources of capital. Accounting fees, legal fees, and prospectus printing and distribution, as well as the cost of underwriting the stock, can result in high costs.

Disclosure – Detailed disclosures of the company's affairs must be made public. New-venture firms often prefer to keep such information private.

Requirements – The paperwork involved with SEC regulations, as well as continuing performance information, drains large amounts of time, energy, and money from management. Many new ventures consider these elements better invested in helping the company grow.

Shareholder pressure – Management decisions are sometimes short term in nature in order to maintain a good performance record for earnings and dividends to the shareholders. This pressure can lead to a failure to give adequate consideration to the company's long-term growth and improvement.

The advantages and disadvantages of going public must be weighed carefully. If the decision is to undertake a public offering, then it is important the entrepreneur understand the process involved.

The mechanics of going public are governed by security laws in each country, but there are some common elements across all countries. [19] Some of these common elements are listed below:

Investor Information – There are requirement levels of firm information that must be given to investors prior to the IPO, like a prospectus. Also, the place of listing or trading of the new shares may also require specific information, like the number of prior years of financial data, etc.

Investment Banker (IB) or underwriter – Most firms select a lead investment banker to sell the new securities. There tends to be somewhat uniform fees (7 percent of the issue value in the U.S.) that are charged the issuing firm by the investment banker. If "book building" is used, the selected IB conducts "road shows" or other type of information gathering activities to measure the demand for the securities at different prices. Underwriter reputation has been shown to affect initial return levels.

Ownership structure – With an IPO, the ownership structure will change. The shares sold in the IPO are designated as Primary shares, which are new shares, and Secondary shares, which are shares that were previously owned by existing shareholders, usually founders and managers of the firm. The size of the new issue relative to the existing shares and their distribution will change the ownership structure. The IPO is often a method of moving from firm founders toward a professional management of the firm. The IPO generally occurs at the end of the "entrepreneurial activities" of the founder, but usually he/she will play a role in the future of the company.

Lock-up provisions – When going public, IPOs almost always commit to a "lock-up period," whereby insiders are prohibited from selling shares without the written permission of the lead underwriter until a certain amount of time has passed. The average is 180 days or 6 months. Obviously, using these lock-up provisions is an attempt to control the supply of shares sold during the period after the IPO by insiders or existing shareholders.

The presence of Venture Capitalists (VC) – Many firms may be financed by VCs who take an ownership position and have partial control over the entrepreneurs. The IPO may change this control as the VC distributes the shares to their limited partners. The use of an IPO may be a cheaper form of financing than provided by VC and will certainly provide liquidity to the existing pre-IPO shareholders.

Issue size – With the fixed costs of an IPO to create a liquid market, the number of new shares in the IPO should be large enough to provide sufficient liquidity, but small enough so that the issuing firm does not raise more cash than it can profitably use.

Mechanism for pricing IPOs – There tends to be three mechanisms used in IPOs around the world: auctions, fixed-priced offers, or book building. In auctions, the market-clearing price is determined after bids are submitted. In a fixed-priced offer, the price has been set prior to the allocation. If there is excess demand, shares are rationed on a pro-rata or lottery basis. In book building, the investment bankers canvas potential buyers and then set an offer price. The predominant mechanism by which IPO shares are sold around the world has become book building.

The prospectus is a formal written offer to sell securities that provides an investor with the necessary information to make an informed decision. If a company is raising capital by offering its shares or other securities to the public for the first time, it will issue a disclosure document called a prospectus. In the UK, for example, a prospectus would be lodged with the financial services section, Securities and Investments of Her Majesty's (HM) Treasury. For further information visit: www.hmtreasury.gov.uk. As part of the work towards the Lisbon agenda and in an attempt to cut the cost of accessing capital for EU firms, especially SMEs, the EU governments aim to implement a new Prospectus Directive. This prospectus should provide an effective passport for issuers – lowering the cost of accessing capital for firms across the EU, and making the EU capital market more efficient and liquid, whilst ensuring that there is an appropriate level of protection which distinguishes between professional and retail investors.

The prospectus must fully disclose all pertinent information about a company and must present a fair representation of the firm's true prospects. All negative information must be clearly highlighted and explained. Some of the specific detailed information that must be presented includes:

- History and nature of the company

- Capital structure

- Description of any material contracts

- Description of securities being registered

- Salaries and security holdings of major officers and directors and the price they paid for holdings

- Underwriting arrangements

- Estimate and use of net proceeds

- Audited financial statements

- Information about the competition with an estimation of the chances of the company's survival.

Going Public: The Acid Test[20]

Here are six questions that will help you see if your company is best suited for the public listing:

Are you building a company that can run without you? The work leading up to a public offering is so intensive that it will take an entrepreneur's focus away from the everyday operations, ultimately hurting the business. Without a strong management team, consider hiring a CFO that has experience taking companies, preferably small, through the rigors of going public.

Can you get to a market capitalisation of within three years of going public? Your financials can answer this question for you. The value of a public company is a multiple of what it earns. Take the average price-earnings ratio for your industry and apply it to the earnings you project for the third year after your company goes public. If the result isn't near $100 million, staying private may be best. This number is a good indicator because it is the level of earnings at which the company can attract brokers and investors.

Are you building a company with high gross and operating margins? A high sales volume will be reached only if the company has access to adequate funding to promote and finance sales. The bottom line truly rests on the top line, and a public company cannot afford to lose its most important number. High margins will help curb any unexpected losses.

Can your business deliver double-digit sales and earnings growth? The competition amongst public companies, mutual funds, and other investment networks is fierce. Investors won't look twice at a company that doesn't grow fast enough to warrant the use of their time and money.

Are you building a family business? If the succession plan for the business is set in stone to be passed on to the kids, don't go public. Families measure the success of a business generation by generation. Money movers are interested in the quarter-to-quarter progress. Going public will eventually be the end of any succession strategy.

Can the business be built inexpensively? The main reason companies go public is to raise initial funds for major growth. As a result, sales and growth need to reflect the use of the first round of financing. If it's perceived that another round of financing will be necessary to achieve the original plan, investors will look elsewhere.

What are private placements?

Private placement is money invested in a company usually from private investors in the form of stocks or sometimes bonds. It is sometimes possible to avoid issuing a prospectus, but rules will differ from country to country. In most cases a placement agent (usually a stock broking firm or investment bank) will manage the process for a fee. In Northern Ireland you should expect to pay £50-350 in fees plus a percentage of any money raised. In the United States, private placement often does not need to be registered with the Securities Exchange Commission under the so-called Regulation D.

The ideal small business candidate for private placement is a company looking for growth or expansion funding. A private placement is suitable when you need an injection of capital to jump to the next level of growth and you have a proven track record of profitability, or at least sales.

A Private Placement Memorandum (PPM) is the document that discloses everything the investors need to know to make an informed investment decision about the Direct Public Offering (DPO) being considered. This includes: the offering structure, the share structure of the company, disclosures about the securities being purchased, company information, information on company operations, risks involved with the investment, management information, use of proceeds, information on certain transactions that could affect the investor, and investor suitability data.[21] The PPM is very important because it provides the investor with all of the prescribed data they will need to make an investment decision and includes the actual documentation to effect the investment transaction.

Advantages of private placements. A key advantage of a placement is that the company has a considerable degree of control over the terms of the placement (who participates, the amount and price of equity issued). Also investors who participate in placements are less likely to want day-to-day control over your operations (unlike some business angels).

Disadvantages of private placements. Private placements can be quite time consuming as you will need to prepare a detailed information memorandum which outlines your business, past performance, future plans and viability. The cost of a placement can be prohibitive, as you will need not only a placement agent, but also accountants and lawyers who are experienced with the process. Another downside of placements is the level of disclosure required. Your vision and detailed plans for the business become known to investors and competitors alike.[22]

It is important that entrepreneurs in each country take advice on the limits of private placement.

Management Buyouts (MBOs)

An MBO is exactly what it says, the buyout of a business from its owners by the existing management team running the business. MBOs afford an opportunity for experienced managers to satisfy their latent entrepreneurial instincts while providing distinctive and unique solution to the vendor's specific requirements. This happens with more expanding entrepreneurial companies, not with start-ups.

Since most managers don't have million euro bank accounts to buy their own businesses, most approach local banks. Banks look for profitability and cash flow.

In Ireland, when the economy is slow, older, unloved and undervalued companies at the lower edge of the Irish and other stock exchanges are tempted targets for MBOs.[23]

Sometimes this happens because of unsuccessful floats. It's called a public to private buyout. The Irish tech sector in particular has also seen a number of companies - such as Alphyra, Riverdeep and Conduit - which had only recently IPOed being taken private again by way of management buyouts.

The key factor in success is motivation. The importance of the entrepreneurial skills of the management team cannot be overemphasized. There are a number of well-documented cases where experienced managers from large, well-reputed organisations have been brought in to run smaller businesses, which required considerable entrepreneurial skills. However, these managers, who are used to more structured organisations, lacked the skills required of entrepreneurs and failed to deliver.[24]

The Venture Capital Market

Venture capitalists are a valuable and powerful source of equity funding for new ventures. These experienced professionals provide a full range of financial services for new or growing ventures, including the following:

- Capital for start-ups and expansion

- Market research and strategy for businesses that do not have their own marketing departments

- Management-consulting functions and management audit and evaluation

- Contacts with prospective customers, suppliers, and other important businesspeople

- Assistance in negotiating technical agreements

- Help in establishing management and accounting controls

- Help in employee recruitment and employee agreements

- Help in risk management and the establishment of an effective insurance program

- Counselling and guidance in complying with a myriad of government regulations.

There are different stages of venture investing:

Seed financing provides the initial funds for a business concept to be developed. This may involve additional research, product development and initial marketing to reach out to early-adopter customers. The companies receiving funding at this stage may be in the process of just being incorporated or may have been in operations for a while.

Early-stage financing is provided to companies that have completed the product development stage and test marketing as well, but require additional financing to expand commercial manufacturing and sales.

Expansion financing is provided when the start-up company is poised to grow rapidly. The business is viable and is reaching break-even point. The funds may be used to increase, production capacity, market or product development, and/or provide additional working capital.

Late-stage funding refers to the pre-IPO investments in a company for the purpose of strengthening the positioning of the company, and gaining endorsements from the top venture capital firms as the company prepares for its listing.

Exit mechanisms

In most venture investments, exit conditions are agreed upon in the term sheet at the time of the investment. There are five main exit mechanisms:

Trade sale to another company – The venture capitalist may not exit completely, but retain some quoted shares if he/she believes further growth is likely.

Repurchase of the venture capitalists' shares by the investee company – Where a company buys back its shares from the investors.

Refinancing or purchase of the venture capitalists' equity by a longer-term investment institution – This is like an investment trust and can occur when the venture capitalist is looking for an exit but the investee company is unwilling to go for a listing or a trade sale.

Stock market listing – Going public allows for the realisation of owner's capital; funds available for expansion; marketable shares available for acquisitions; enhancement of status and public awareness; and increased employee motivation via share incentive schemes.

Involuntary exit – this can occur through receivership or liquidation.

Recent developments in venture capital

The trend in classic venture capital investment turned upward in 2004 for the first time since 2000 when the Internet bubble burst and wreaked havoc with the portfolios of many venture capital firms.[25] In the US, classic venture capital investment plunged from its all-time peak of $105.8 billion in 2000 to $18.9 billion in 2003, then rose to $21 billion in 2004. In Europe, the amount of classic venture capital investment increased from $10.2 billion to $12.5 billion from 2003 to 2004.

The strong upturn has also been apparent in Ireland and the United Kingdom, measured in absolute terms, in percentage of GDP, and in per company amounts. However, venture capitalists on both sides are retrenching and being more cautious as seen in the strong drops in the number of companies receiving VC (see Table 7).

What are Venture Capitalists looking for?

Venture capitalists are particularly interested in making large returns on investments. Table 8 provides some commonly sought targets. Of course, these targets are flexible. They would be reduced in cases where a company has a strong market potential, is able to generate good cash flow, or the management has invested a sizable portion of its own funds in the venture.[26] However, an annual goal of 20-30 percent return on investment would not be considered too high, regardless of the risks involved.

Table 7 Venture capital in Ireland and the United Kingdom

Classic VC Invested domestically € (1,000)			
	2002	2003	2004
Ireland	€204,416	€64,217	€169,864
United Kingdom	€1,751,946	€1,371,583	€1,873,920
Classic VC Invested domestically percent GDP			
	2002	2003	2004
Ireland	0.057	0.061	0.112
United Kingdom	0.089	0.101	0.105
Classic VC invested per domestic company US$ (1,000)			
	2002	2003	2004
Ireland	€624	€1,406	€2,421
United Kingdom	€1,305	€1,206	€2,026
Number of domestic Companies Receiving Classic VC			
	2002	2003	2004
Ireland	152	122	70
United Kingdom	1,343	1,137	924
Source: Bill Bygrave, Babson College, and *Global Entrepreneurship Monitor* 2005. USD converted to Euros using respective year values.			

Table 8 Returns typically sought by venture capitalists

Stage of business	Expected percentage annual Return on Investment (ROI %)	Expected Increase on Initial Investment
Start-up business (idea stage)	60 +	10–15 X investment
First-stage financing (new business)	40–60	6–12 X investment
Second-stage financing (development stage)	30–50	4–8 X investment
Third-stage financing (expansion stage)	25–40	3–6 X investment
Turnaround situation	50 +	8–15 X investment

Dos and don'ts of approaching venture capitalists[27]

Venture capitalists are busy people, constantly inundated with business plans that range from pipe dreams to the next software giant. Keep these things in mind if you want to capture their attention.

Do

Prepare all materials before soliciting firms

Send a business plan and cover letter first

Solicit several firms

Keep phone conversations brief – have a 1-minuter and a 3-minuter

Remain positive and enthusiastic about your company, product, and service

Know your minimum deal and walk away if necessary

Negotiate a deal you can live with

Investigate the venture capitalist's previous deals and current portfolio structure

Don't

Expect a response

Dodge questions

Give vague answers – know what you can and cannot disclose before you start talking so that you do not stumble over awkward questions

Don't switch off – be an active listener you will always learn something

Hide significant problems

Expect immediate decisions

Fixate on pricing

Embellish facts or projections

Bring your lawyer

How Venture Capitalists evaluate venture proposals

Considering venture capitalists receive many proposals, some level of screening is necessary. Researchers have discovered that venture capitalists reached a "go/no go" decision in an average of 6 minutes on the initial screening and less than 21 minutes on the overall proposal evaluation. They found that the venture capital firm's requirements and the long-term growth and profitability of the proposed venture's industry were the critical factors for initial screening. In the more-detailed evaluation, the backgrounds of the entrepreneurs as well as the characteristics of the proposal itself were important for further consideration.[28] In a study examining the "demand side" of venture capital, researchers surveyed 318 private entrepreneurs who sought out venture capital in amounts of $100,000 or more. The study found that entrepreneurs' success with acquiring funding is related to four general categories: (1) characteristics of the entrepreneurs, including education, experience, and age; (2) characteristics of the enterprise, including stage, industry type, and location (for example, rural or urban); (3) characteristics of the request, including amount, business plan, and prospective capital source; and (4) sources of advice, including technology, preparation of the business plan, and places to seek funding.

The business plan is a critical element in a new-venture proposal and should be complete, clear, and well presented. Venture capitalists will generally analyse five major aspects of the plan: (1) the proposal size, (2) financial projections, (3) investment recovery, (4) competitive advantage, and (5) company management.

Figure 2 portrays the key screening criterion for VCs.

In addition to initial screening venture capitalists seek to evaluate product ideas and management strategies. Researchers suggest there are numerous criteria used by venture capitalists to evaluate new-venture proposals.[29] A list of eight critical attributes that venture capitalists use to evaluate if they will invest or not are exhibited in Table 9. The level at which the attribute applies and its definition are also provided.

In a study examining the "demand side" of venture capital, researchers surveyed 318 private entrepreneurs who sought out venture capital in amounts of $100,000 or more. The study found that entrepreneurs' success with acquiring funding is related to four general categories: (1) characteristics of the entrepreneurs, including education, experience, and age; (2) characteristics of the enterprise, including stage, industry type, and location (for example, rural or urban); (3) characteristics of the request, including amount, business plan, and prospective capital source; and (4) sources of advice, including technology, preparation of the business plan, and places to seek funding.[30]

The business plan is a critical element in a new-venture proposal and should be complete, clear, and well presented. Venture capitalists will generally analyse five major aspects of the plan: (1) the proposal size, (2) financial projections, (3) investment recovery, (4) competitive advantage, and (5) company management.

Figure 2 Venture Capitalists' Screening Criteria

Venture Capital Firm Requirements

- Must fit within lending guidelines for stage/size of investment

- Proposed business must be within geographic area of interest

- Prefer proposals from someone known to venture capitalist firm

- Proposed industry is type of industry invested in by venture

Nature of the Proposed Business

- Projected growth is relatively large within five years of investment

- Economic environment of proposed industry

- Industry must be capable of long-term growth and profitability

- Economic environment should be favourable to a new entrant

Proposed Business Strategy

- Selection of distribution channel(s) must be feasible

- Product must demonstrate defendable competitive position

- Financial Information on the proposed business should be realistic

Proposal Characteristics

- Must have full information

- Reasonable length, concise, easy to scan, professionally presented

- Proposal must contain a balanced presentation

- Use graphics and large print to emphasize key points

Entrepreneur/Team Characteristics

- Must have relevant experience

- Appropriate length, concise, easy to scan, professionally presented

- Should have a balanced management team in place

- Management must be willing to work with venture partners

- Serial/portfolio entrepreneurs are given special consideration.

Table 9 Attributes in venture capitalists' evaluation process

Attribute	Level	Definition
Timing of entry	Pioneer	Enters a new industry first
	Late follower	Enters an industry late in the industry's stage of development
Key success factor stability	High	Requirements necessary for success will not change radically during industry development
	Low	Requirements necessary for success will change radically during industry development
Educational capability	High	Considerable resources and skills available to overcome market ignorance through education
	Low	Few resources or skills available to overcome market ignorance through education
Lead time	Long	An extended period of monopoly for the first entrant prior to competitors entering the industry
	Short	A minimal period of monopoly for the first entrant prior to competitors entering this industry
Competitive rivalry	High	Intense competition amongst industry members during industry development
	Low	Little competition amongst industry members during industry development
Entry wedge mimicry	High	Considerable imitation of the mechanisms used by other firms to enter this, or any other, industry—for example, a franchisee
	Low	Minimal imitation of the mechanisms used by other firms to enter this, or any other, industry—for example, introducing a new product
Scope	Broad	A firm that spreads its resources across a wide spectrum of the market – for example, many segments of the market
	Narrow	A firm that concentrates on intensively exploiting a small segment of the market—for example, targeting a niche
Industry-related competence	High	Venturer has considerable experience and knowledge with the industry being entered on a related industry
	Low	Venturer has minimal experience and knowledge with the industry being entered or related industry

Stages of the evaluation process

The evaluation process typically takes place in stages. The four most common stages follow.

Stage 1: Initial screening – This is a quick review of the basic venture to see if it meets the venture capitalist's particular interests.

Stage 2: Evaluation of the business plan – This is where a detailed reading of the plan is done in order to evaluate the factors mentioned earlier.

Stage 3: Oral presentation – The entrepreneur verbally presents the plan to the venture capitalist.

Stage 4: Final evaluation – After analysing the plan and visiting with suppliers, customers, consultants, and others, the venture capitalist makes a final decision.

This four-step process screens out approximately 98 percent of all venture plans. The rest receive some degree of financial backing.

How entrepreneurs can evaluate the venture capitalist

The venture capitalist will evaluate the entrepreneur's proposal carefully, and the entrepreneur should not hesitate to evaluate the venture capitalist. Does the venture capitalist understand the proposal? Is the individual familiar with the business? Is the person someone with whom the entrepreneur can work? If the answers reveal a poor fit, it is best for the entrepreneur to look for a different venture capitalist.

One researcher found that venture capitalists *do* add value to an entrepreneurial firm beyond the money they supply, especially in high-innovation ventures. Because of this finding, entrepreneurs need to choose the appropriate venture capitalist at the outset and, most importantly, they must keep the communication channels open as the firm grows.[31]

On the other hand, it is important to realize that the choice of a venture capitalist can be limited. Although funds are available today, they tend to be controlled by fewer groups, and the quality of the venture must be promising. In addition, the trend toward concentration of venture capital under the control of a few firms is increasing.[32]

Asking venture capitalist the right questions[33]

There are a number of important questions that entrepreneurs should ask of venture capitalists. Here are seven of the most important along with their rationales.

Does the venture capital firm in fact invest in your industry? How many deals has the firm actually done in your field?

What is it like to work with this venture capital firm? Get references. (An unscreened list of referrals, including CEOs of companies that the firm has been successful with as well as those it has not, can be very helpful.)

What experience does the partner doing your deal have, and what is his or her clout within the firm? Check out the experiences of other entrepreneurs.

How much time will the partner spend with your company if you run into trouble? A seed-stage company should ask, "You guys are a big fund, and you say you can seed me a quarter of a million euros. How often will you be able to see me?" The answer should be at least once a week.

How healthy is the venture capital fund, and how much has been invested? A venture firm with a lot of troubled investments will not have much time to spare. If most of the fund is invested, there may not be much money available for your follow-on rounds.

Are the investment goals of the venture capitalists consistent with your own? If they are not aligned to your own you need to make sure of the reasons why the venture firm is investing in your business and hoe you can better match the investment goals to prevent conflict at a later stage.

Have the venture firm and the partner championing your deal been through any economic downturns? A good venture capitalist won't panic when things get bad so this can be a good indication of how they will treat you when you do not meet set targets.

Angel Financing

Not all venture capital is raised through formal sources such as public and private placements. Many wealthy people are looking for investment opportunities. They are referred to as business angels. Here we distinguish "business angels" from the 4F's informal investors—friends, family, founders, and other "foolhardy" investors—that we looked at the beginning of the book (see "Finding Informal Investment" above). Figure 3 below recaps where angels fit in the mix.

Figure 3 Where angels fit in the mix

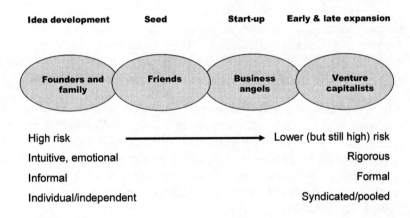

How big is the angel capital market? Studies in the US and Scandinavia suggest that the angel capital market is probably about ten times the size of the venture capital market. [34] Mason and Harrison estimate that angel capital investment in the UK is broadly equivalent to the amount of institutional venture capital provided to start-up and early stage ventures.[35] They also point out that the smaller average size of investments in the informal venture capital market is reflected in the fact that eight times as many businesses raise finance from business angels than from institutional venture capital funds.

Business angels are active, in one way or another, in every country worldwide. To illustrate, the early expansion of the Body Shop was supported by an investment through a business angel whose £4,000 investment was worth in excess of £140 million in the early 1990s. Business angels tend not to have any previous relationship with the entrepreneur, and therefore take a more objective approach to determining whether or not to invest. Angel investors range from those taking a passive approach (backing others' judgments), through to hands-on investors providing advice or direct management input to help the business become established. In many cases the latter group of angel investors will take as rigorous an approach to their investing as some venture capitalists. A key difference between angel and venture investors is that angels tend to invest as individuals (often as part of a group) operating part-time, whereas venture capital generally comes via a company or fund with full-time managers and a board, using formal analysis and investment procedures.

An angel investor is defined as someone who has already made his or her money and now seeks out promising young ventures to support financially. "Angels are typically entrepreneurs, retired corporate executives, or professionals who have a net worth of more than $100,000 a year. They are self-starters. Business angels are trying to perpetuate the system that made them successful."[36] If entrepreneurs are looking for such an angel, Wetzel advises them, "Don't look very far away—within 50 miles or within a day's drive at most. And that's because this is not a full-time profession for them."[37]

Why would individuals be interested in investing in a new venture from which professional venture capitalists see no powerful payoff? It may be, of course, that the reduced investment amount reduces the total risk involved in the investment. However, informal investors seek other non-financial returns, amongst them the creation of jobs in areas of high unemployment; development of technology for social needs (for example, medical or energy); local revitalisation; and personal satisfaction from assisting entrepreneurs.[38]

Table 10 describes the major differences between business angels and venture capitalists.[39]

Table 10 Differences between Angels and Venture Capitalists

Differential factor	Investor type	
	Business Angels	Venture Capitalists
Personal	Entrepreneurs	Investors
Firms funded	Small, early-stage	Large, mature
Due diligence done	Minimal	Extensive
Location of investment	Of concern	Not important
Contract used	Simple	Comprehensive
Monitoring after investment	Active, hands-on	Strategic
Exiting the firm	Of lesser concern	Highly important
Rate of return	Of lesser concern	Highly important

Angel investors in the island of Ireland

How do informal investors find projects? Research studies indicate that they use a network of friends. Additionally, many localities are formulating venture capital networks, which attempt to link informal investors with entrepreneurs and their new or growing ventures.

The Northern Ireland Business Angel Network through its *halo* network assists entrepreneurs in identifying the best source of angel financing for each individual business. Whilst *halo* recognises that most Business Angels find their prospective partners by chance or through previous business contacts, *halo* aims to make the match more efficient, effective and right for you. The Network is an initiative from Investment Belfast, designed to match and introduce investors to potential entrepreneurs. Clients are generally highly enthusiastic but not investor ready. Business angles wishing to invest through the network must contribute financial support and be experienced in acting as a business advisor to support high growth businesses in Northern Ireland. For more information visit: www.haloni.com or the UK equivalent National Business Angels Network at www.nban.co.uk.

Synergy 2000 is another business angel network operating through Lisburn Enterprise Organisation but across Northern Ireland and the border counties to match businesses with private investors in different sectors. For more information visit: www.lisburn-enterprise.co.uk. Regarding information for support available for social entrepreneurs, it may be worthwhile checking out the Social Economy Network, visit:

http://www.socialeconomynetwork.org /support.asp. SEN has offices in Derry, Northern Ireland and has a list of the local area partnerships that can often provide financial assistance and asset building. For specific cash flow problems there are factoring services available through companies such as Ulster Factors Limited that was established as early as 1969 as the first factoring company in Ireland. You can make email enquiries to Enquiries@ulsterfactors.com. There is also a centre for Co-operative Studies in University College Cork in Ireland (visit: www.ucc.ie) that aims to promote, through its research, consultancy and educational activities, the continued growth of the co-operative movement, as an effective, locally-owned and democratically-controlled sector of the economy. This Centre could provide useful advice for links with other similar businesses to form clusters and networks for financial or other reasons.

There a number of additional business angel networks in the UK, a few of which are exemplified here. Business Angel Ventures (BAC Ventures) is a joint project of Business Angel Capital Limited and The Venture Site Limited, aiming to bring about the best in venture capital fundraising on the UK business angel market from commercial and private investors. Examples of projects on their portfolio are diverse and include 3-D imaging technology, new film production, unique cyclists and sport safety helmet and mobile content provider. For more information visit: www.bacventures.co.uk. Angel Investment Network is a network offering leading edge technology and more traditional business proposals. Examples include Communications, entertainment, construction and education. For more information visit: www.angelinvestmentnetwork.co.uk

Another example across the island of Ireland is the EquityNetwork organised through InterTrade Ireland to assist businesses in becoming 'investor ready' and providing signposting for equity financing. For more information visit: www.intertradeireland.com

Though angel investing has both its advantages and disadvantages, it is widely agreed that the advantages of business angels generally outweigh their disadvantages, making an active informal venture capital market a prerequisite for a vigorous enterprise economy.[40]

Types of Angel Investors

Angel investors can be classified into five basic groups:

Corporate angels – Typically, so-called corporate angels are senior managers at who have been laid off with generous severances or have taken early retirement. In addition to receiving the cash, an entrepreneur may persuade the corporate angel to occupy some senior management position, such as in business development.

Entrepreneurial angels – The most prevalent type of investors, most of these individuals own and operate highly successful businesses. Because these investors have other sources of income, and perhaps significant wealth from IPOs or partial buyouts, they will take bigger risks and invest more capital. The best way to market your deal to these angels, therefore, is as a synergistic opportunity. Reflecting this orientation, entrepreneurial angels seldom look at companies outside of their own area of expertise and will participate in no more than a handful of investments at any one time. These investors almost always take a seat on the board of directors but rarely assume management duties. They will make fair-sized investments and invest more as the company progresses.

Enthusiast angels – Whereas entrepreneurial angels tend to be somewhat calculating, enthusiasts simply like to be involved in deals. Most enthusiast angels are age 65 or older, are independently wealthy from success in a business they started, and have abbreviated work schedules. For them, investing is a hobby. As a result, they typically play no role in management and rarely seek to be placed on a board. Because they spread themselves across so many companies, the size of their investments tends to be small.

Micromanagement angels – Micromanagers are very serious investors. Some of them were born wealthy, but the vast majority attained wealth through their own efforts. Unfortunately, this heritage makes them dangerous. Because most have successfully built a company, micromanagers attempt to impose the tactics that worked for them on their portfolio companies. Although they do not seek an active management role, micromanagers usually demand a seat on the board of directors. If business is not going well, they will try to bring in new managers.

Professional angels – The term "professional" in this context refers to the investor's occupation, such as doctor, lawyer and, in some very rare instances, accountant. Professional angels like to invest in companies that offer a product or service with which they have some experience. They rarely seek a board seat, but they can be unpleasant to deal with when the going gets rough and may believe that a company is in trouble before it actually is. Professional angels will invest in several companies at one time.[41]

Obviously, informal networks are a major potential capital source for entrepreneurs. However, every entrepreneur should be careful and thorough in his/her approach to business angels. There are advantages and disadvantages associated with "angel financing". The list below illustrates some of the critical pros and cons of dealing with business angels. It is only through recognition of these issues that entrepreneurs will be able to establish the best relationship with a business angel.

Advantages and Disadvantages of Business Angels

Advantages

Business angels prefer funding high-risk entrepreneurial firms in their earliest stages being the major source of external funds for start-ups with high growth potential. Business angels fill the so-called equity gap by making their investments exactly in those areas in which institutional venture capital providers are reluctant to invest.

Business angels prefer funding the small amounts (falling within the equity gap) needed to launch new ventures.

Business angels make investments in virtually all industry sectors. Sector aside, however, it should be noted that what most attracts angels to an investment is high growth potential.

Business angels are more flexible in their financial decisions than venture capitalists and tend to have different investment criteria, longer investment horizons ("patient money"), shorter investment processes, and lower targeted rates of return.

Raising funds from business angels does not involve the high fees incurred when raising funding from financial institutions.

Most business angels are value-added investors in that they contribute their personal business skills to furthering young businesses and therefore may elect to invest locally to facilitate involvement. This free assistance and advice from an investor who, quite often, is a seasoned veteran of the business world is priceless for young entrepreneurs starting out and would not normally be affordable by other means.

The business angel financing market is more geographically dispersed than the formal venture capital market; business angels can be found everywhere, not just in major financial centres.

Obtaining money from a business angel has a leveraging effect in that it makes the investee firm more attractive to other sources of possible finance. Angel investments certainly heighten venture capital interest in such ventures.

Business angels are also instrumental thanks to the loan guarantees they offer their investee firms, in addition to the money they personally invest.

Angels are not averse to funding technology companies, which inherently come with high risks.

Disadvantages

Business angels are less likely to make follow-on investments in the same firm. Conversely, venture capitalists spend around two-thirds of their funds on expansion funding of their existing portfolio firms.

Business angels prefer to have a say in the running of the firm, which may force the entrepreneur to give up some degree of control. Some business angels may have limited expertise in running the particular type of investee firm they fund, making their contribution less value-added and more meddlesome.

A small minority of business angels may turn out to be "devils" that have self-serving motives for investment, rather than promoting the good of the firm.

Unlike many venture capital firms, business angels do not have the national reputation and prestige of a big-name institution, which can be crucial if the firm is successful enough to seek assistance from an investment bank for a private placement or IPO. Figure 4 below summarises the advantages and disadvantages of business angel investment.

Figure 4 The pros and cons of business angel investment

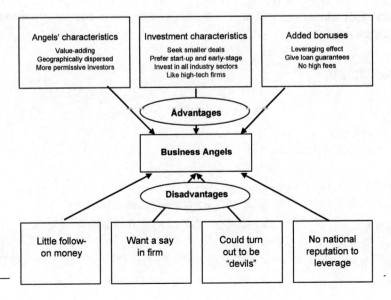

Irish Venture Capital and Private Equity Funds

Finally we get to the most valuable part of this book. For entrepreneurs it is often said "Know who is more important than know how". This material is part adopted from the Irish Venture Capital Association (IVCA) and InterTrade Ireland's Equity Network 2004/05 edition and the follow-up Third edition. IVCA was established in 1985 and is the representative body of the venture capital and private equity industry on the island. It provides signposting to equity for the benefit of entrepreneurs, corporate financiers, investors and practitioners (lawyers and bankers). IVCA manages over 95 percent of the funds under management and seeks to improve understanding of the requirements in a business proposition and to improve performance and professional standards of member firms and the individuals within those firms.

Research carried out by InterTrade Ireland's EquityNetwork in 1999 revealed a dramatic increase in the amounts of private equity raised and invested in the previous decade with some regional variations. The research highlighted a gap in the supply of equity finance to the high-risk early stage projects. During the five-year period, 1999-2003 IVCA members invested €833 million in over 700 companies. These funds have different investment criteria with various sector, geographical and stage of investment preferences. At present it is estimated that over €200 million is available for investment in early stage or in existing companies seeking to expand.

The following material highlights the extent of venture capital and private equity funds available on the island of Ireland and denotes how entrepreneurs can make contact with investors should their needs meet particular funding criteria.

3i Group plc

Category:	Venture Capital & Private Equity
Contacts:	Dr Dina Chaya, Director London UK
Tel:	+44 (0) 20 7928 3131
Fax:	+44 (0) 20 7928 0058
Email:	london@3i.com
Web:	www.3i.com/contacts/london.html
Address:	91 Waterloo Road, London SE1 8XP
Investment range: Up to €150M	
Total funds:	€1.3bn/ year

Sectors: Broad range for private equity. Venture capital sectors include healthcare, software, communications and electronics.

Summary: Active across all stages of funding and a range of sectors and geographical markets, from early-stage venture capital (range €2m to €50m) to growth capital (€10m and €150m) and buyouts (up to €1bn). There are 250 investment professionals spanning three continents, linking us to a wealth of corporate contacts and industry experts, giving both a local and global view of industry trends. UK/Ireland companies in their portfolio include Hobbs (designer, manufacturer and retailer of contemporary womenswear) and JP Corry Group is a holding company for four major trading operations: In north and south of Ireland including the largest building merchants based in Northern Ireland.

Note for buy-ins and late stage development capital in the range of £25M to £130M, contact Alchemy Partners for private equity (www.alchemypartners.com). They have invested £1.5bn since January 1997 and their portfolio contains many previously public companies that have turned private. The fund is derived from high quality blue chip investors including major banks and universities.

ACT Venture Capital

Category:	Venture Capital
Contacts:	Niall Carroll, MD
Tel:	+353 (0) 1 260 0966
Fax:	+353 (0) 1 260 0538
Email:	info@actvc.ie
Web:	www.actventure.com
Address:	Richview Office Park, Clonskeagh, Dublin 14
Investment range:	€750,000-15M
Total funds:	€300M

Sectors: Information and communications, technologies, medical devices and life sciences

Summary: ACT's funds are sourced in both domestic and international financial institutions. Investments are made in companies at all stages of their growth but there is particular interest in early-stage companies. ACT is highly active in supporting companies through international expansion.

Alliance Investment Capital

Category:	Venture Capital
Contacts:	Frank Traynor, MD
Tel:	+353 (0) 1 283 7656
Fax:	+353 (0) 1 283 7256
Email:	frank.traynor@allinv.com
Web:	www.alliance.ie

Address:	CFI House, Clonskeagh Square, Dublin 14
Investment range:	€500,000-2M
Total funds:	€9.5M
Sectors:	All

Summary: The first Alliance Investment Capital Venture Fund was launched in 1999. Limited partners are Royal Bank of Scotland Private Equity and Enterprise Ireland. The fund has invested in 5 companies and is currently closed for further investments.

Anglo Irish Capital Partners

Category:	Private Equity
Contacts:	Pat Walsh, MD
Tel:	+353 (0) 1 616 2705
Fax:	+353 (0) 1 616 2895
Email:	patwalsh@angloirishbank.ie
Web:	www.angloirishbank.ie
Address:	61 Fitzwilliam Square Dublin 2
Investment range:	€500,000-2M
Total funds:	€15M
Sectors:	All

Summary: Equity capital provided for development capital, management buy-outs/buyins and shareholder release. They operate in a number of industry sectors including construction, office investment, hotels, retails, public houses, leisure and manufacturing.

BOI Kernel Capital Partners Private Equity Fund

Category:	Private Equity
Contacts:	Niall Olden, MD
Tel:	+353 (0) 21 482 6030
Fax:	+353 (0) 21 482 6034
Email:	niall.olden@kernelcapital.ie
Web:	www.kernelcapital.ie
Address:	Unit 4 Westpoint Buildings Westpoint Business Park, Ballincollig, Cork
Investment range:	€300,000-1.5M
Total funds:	€19M
Sectors:	All except property

Summary: The fund invests in companies at all stages of development. From High Potential Start Ups to more mature MBO and MBI opportunities. The maximum investment per company is €3M. This fund considers supporting high potential 'pilot projects' on case by case basis.

BOI Venture Capital Limited (BOIVC)

Category:	Venture Capital
Contacts:	Brendan Vaughan, Fund Manager
Tel:	+353 (0) 1 665 3443
Fax:	+353 (0) 1 665 3484
Email:	Brendan.Vaughan@boimail.com
Web:	www.boi.ie/venturecapital
Address:	40 Mespil Road Dublin 4
Investment range:	Up to €2M
Total funds:	€19M
Sectors:	ICT

Summary: Dublin based fund with regional offices in Tullamore, Galway, Limerick and Cork. BoI Venture Capital Limited (BOIVC) seeks to invest in companies with strong management teams, sound business models, defensible competitive advantages and internationally traded products. BOIVC will either act as the sole sponsor or lead, co-lead or participate in a syndicate. Investment exits are typically targeted to occur within 4-7 years, but flexible time horizons are maintained to maximize investment return

Corporate Finance Ireland Limited

Category:	Private Equity
Contacts:	James Mc Carthy, Fund Manager
Tel:	+353 (0) 1 283 7144
Fax:	+353 (0) 1 283 7256
Email:	james.mccarthy@cfi.ie
Web:	www.cfi.ie

Address: CFI House Clonskeagh Square Dublin 14

Sectors: Broad range including technology, life sciences, travel and leisure, motor industry and wind farms.

Summary: Founded in 1987, Corporate Finance Ireland Ltd. is a Dublin based, independent, corporate finance firm offering sophisticated financial advice and fundraising experience. Since its formation CFI has completed in excess of 100 major fund raising transactions ranging from less than €1m to over €150m, across a wide variety of sectors. CFI specialises in MBOs, Fundraising, Mergers and Acquisitions and joint Ventures and Strategic Alliances. CFI Equity Fund Ltd, a sister company of CFI manages the €9.5m Alliance Investment Capital Fund.

Campus Companies Venture Capital Fund

Category: Venture Capital
Contacts: Patrick Ryan, Chief Executive
Tel: +353 (0) 1 449 3200
Fax: +353 (0) 1 449 3299
Email: info@campuscapital.com
Web: www.campuscapital.com
Address: Molesworth House, 8/9 Molesworth Street, Dublin 2
Investment range: €100,000-600,000
Total funds: €7.6M

Sectors: Information Technology, Communications, Internet, Electronics, Bio-technology, Medical – Other, Consumer goods and other

Summary: The fund specialises in seed and early stage for companies registered in Ireland and promoted by graduates of Irish Universities.

Cresent Capital

Category: Venture Capital
Contacts: Colin Walsh, MD
Tel: +44 (0) 28 9023 3633
Fax: +44 (0) 28 9032 9525
Email: mail@cresentcapital.co.uk
Web: www.cresentcapital.co.uk
Address: 5 Cresent Gardens, Belfast BT7 1NS
Investment range: £250,000-750,000
Total funds: €14M

Sectors: Manufacturing, tradable services and IT in Northern Ireland

Summary: One half of funding allocated to expansion funding of younger companies. The balance of the fund is allocated to development capital for mature companies, MBOs and MBIs.

Cross Atlantic Capital Partners

Category: Venture Capital
Contacts: Gerry Mc Crory, Managing Director (Founder of Crucible Corporation visit: www.cruiciblecorp.com)
Tel: +353 (1) 664 1721
Fax: +353 (1) 664 1806
Email: info@xacp.com

Web: www.xacp.com

Address: Alexandra House, The Sweepstakes, Ballsbridge, Dublin 4

Investment range: $2m to $10m

Total funds: €270M

Sectors: Broadband Communications, Mobile Communications, E-Business Technologies, Nanomaterials Technologies

Summary: Cross Atlantic Capital Partners (XACP) operates several venture funds with over $600 million under management. Portfolio companies, include: Arantech, Auomsoft, Marrakech, MobileAware, Telecom and Gain.

Delta Partners

Category: Venture Capital

Contacts: Frank Kenny, Managing Partner

Tel: +353 (0) 1 294 0870

Fax: +353 (0) 1 294 0877

Email: frank@delta.ie

Web: www.delta.ie

Address: Fujitsu Building, South County Business Park, Leopardstown, Dublin 18

Investment range: £1/2M +

Total funds: €130M

Sectors: Communications technology, software and life sciences

Summary: Delta Partners invests in Ireland and the United Kingdom. It was established in 1994. The firm has a strong focus on investing in early stage technology companies in varied sectors as above. They generally prefer investments to be well positioned in new and very rapidly growing markets where the customers have great enthusiasm for the company's products. Ideally, the product or service takes advantage of a growing market rather than displacing well-established competitors. They like to invest as early as possible in the life cycle of a venture. Most investments are at start-up or within 6-12 months of start-up. Most of Delta's investee companies have intellectual property underpinning the differentiation of their products. Delta does invest in technology-enabled service businesses where speed and quality of execution can lead to a market-winning position without the consumption of significant amounts of capital.

Enterprise Equity Venture Capital Group (Ireland)

Category: Venture Capital

Contacts: Conor O'Connor, CEO

Tel: +353 (0) 42 933 3167

Fax: +353 (0) 42 933 4857

Email: info@enterpriseequity.ie

Web: www.enterpriseequity.ie

Address: Dublin Road Dundalk, Co Louth & Mervue Business Park, Galway

Investment range: €150,000-1,250,000

Total funds: €25M

Sectors: All sectors in Border, midlands and the west region with the exception of property retail and hotels

Summary: Established by the International Fund for Ireland, IFI in 1987. They are commercial providers of Venture Capital to new and expanding business in Northern Ireland and the Border, Midland, Western Region and South Western. Their objective is to stimulate viable and self-sustaining growth in the private sector of the economy. This is achieved through the investment of equity capital in well managed, innovative and growth orientated companies. They have established two venture capital funds on a joint venture basis with Enterprise Ireland. First a €15M fund aimed at established growth-orientated companies; secondly, a €7M seed capital fund aimed at early stage technology companies.

Enterprise Equity Venture Capital Group (No. Ireland)

Category: Venture Capital

Contacts: Aidan Langan, CEO

Tel: +44 (0) 28 9024 2500

Fax: +44 (0) 28 9024 2487

Email: info@eeni.com

Web: www.eeni.com

Address: 78a Dublin Road, Belfast BT2 7HP

Investment range: Up to £2M

Total funds: £16M

Sectors: High growth sectors throughout Northern Ireland

Summary: Established by the International Fund for Ireland, IFI. Enterprise Equity Venture Capital Group is an Ireland wide venture capital organisation with £40 million under management. The Group has offices in Belfast, Dundalk, Galway and Cork. Enterprise Equity (NI) is the Belfast based arm of the group. It has an investment record in a broad spectrum of industry sectors including both technology businesses such as BCO Technologies Ltd, as well as traditional industries such as Ben Sherman. Enterprise Equity backs growth-oriented companies at various stages of their development not only through investment but also by actively working with the key management staff.

Enterprise 2000 Fund

Category:	Venture Capital
Contacts:	Clare Shine/Laurence Enderson, Fund Manager
Tel:	+353 (0) 1 665 3494
Fax:	+353 (0) 1 665 3482
Email:	clare.shine@boimail.com
Address:	40 Mespil Road, Dublin 4
Investment range:	N/A
Total funds:	€13M
Sectors:	Fund fully invested

Summary: This seed capital fund was established in 1998 as a result of a partnership between Bank of Ireland and Enterprise Ireland, it is now fully invested. Funding is available for follow on investments where appropriate.

EVP Early Stage Technology Fund

Category:	Private Equity
Contacts:	Gerry Jones, Partner
Tel:	+353 (0) 1 213 0711
Fax:	+353 (0) 1 213 0515
Email:	gerry.jones@evp.ie
Web:	www.evp.ie
Address:	Arena House, Arena Road Sandyford Industrial Estate, Dublin 18
Investment range:	€300,000-700,000
Total funds:	€5M
Sectors:	ICT

Summary: The fund invests in early stage High Potential Start-ups (HPSUs). EVP has a comprehensive range of services that covers virtually every start-up aspect, from finance, through investor relations to sales and marketing, channel advice, Enterprise Ireland relations and risk reduction.

Glanbia Enterprise Fund

Category:	Private Equity
Contacts:	Joe Doddy, Manager of Innovation Services
Tel:	+353 (0) 1 660 9313
Fax:	+353 (0) 1 660 7904
Email:	dealman@eircom.net

Web: www.glanbiaenterprisefund.com

Address: 74 Pembroke Road, Ballsbridge, Dublin 4

Investment range: Up to €750,000

Total funds: €6.3M

Sectors: Food and Beverage

Summary: The fund is dedicated to investing in emerging food companies at all stages of the business cycle. They have a particular interest in projects involved in food ingredients, nutritional food products and consumer foods but will also consider investments in technologies. Direct funding is provided by way of minority equity investment of up to €750,000. There is access to other sources of capital also to invest in larger projects and subsequent rounds. Enterprise Ireland and Glanbia finance it.

Growcorp GroupLimited

Category: Venture Capital

Contacts: Michael Donnelly, CEO

Tel: +353 (0) 1 466 1000

Fax: +353 (0) 1 466 1002

Email: grow@growcorp.net

Web: www.growcorp.net

Address: 3015 Lake Drive City West Campus, Dublin 24

Investment range: €100,000-1.27M

Total funds: €12.7M

Sectors: Life Sciences

Summary: Growcorp is a leading integrated bioscience investment, advisory and incubation organisation. It was the first private company in Ireland with an investment fund targeted specifically at the bioscience sector ("The European Bioscience Fund I"). They invest at an early stage in amounts up to €1.27M and have led syndicates in excess of €5M for more advanced businesses. The Growcorp team works with entrepreneurs to get their business from start-up to commercial reality through a range of services from strategy optimisation, IP exploitation to fundraising and team building advice.

Hibernia Capital Partners Limited

Category: Venture Capital

Contacts: David Gavagan, Senior Partner

Tel: +353 (0) 1 205 7770

Fax: +353 (0) 1 205 7771

Email: equity@hcp.ie

Web: www.hcp.ie

Address:	Beech House, Beech Hill Office Campus, Clonskeagh, Dublin 4
Investment range:	Up to €16M
Total funds:	€77M
Sectors:	General and in north and south of Ireland

Summary: Part of Trinity Venture Capital group (See above)

Hot Origin

Category:	Venture Capital
Contacts:	David Dalton, CEO
Tel:	+353 (1) 678 8480
Fax:	+353 (1) 678 8477
Email:	ventures@hotorigin.com
Web:	www.hotorigin.com
Address:	64 Lower Mount Street Dublin 2 Ireland
Investment range:	€100,000-€300,000M
Total funds:	€4.1M
Sectors:	Technology particularly those that are in software infrastructure

Summary: HotOrigin is as an equity investor in start-up and first round fund raising, investing up to €320,000. HotOrigin most recent investments in their portfolio include Similarity Systems and Prime Carrier.

ICC Venture Capital

Category:	Venture Capital
Contacts:	Joe Concannon, Investment Director
Tel:	+353 (0) 1 415 5555
Fax:	+353 (0) 1 408 3516
Email:	info@bankofscotland.ie
Web:	www.iccvc.ie
Address:	72-74 Harcourt Street Dublin 2
Investment range:	€ 1M-10M
Total funds:	€230M
Sectors:	General

Summary: The fund targets companies with high growth potential operating in Ireland.

ION Equity Limited

Category:	Venture Capital
Contacts:	Neil O'Leary, Chairman & CEO
Tel:	+353 (0) 1 611 0500

Fax:	+353 (0) 1 611 0510
Email:	info@ionequity.com
Web:	www.ionequity.com
Address:	Fitzwilton House, Wilton Place, Dublin 2
Investment range:	€ 500,000-1M
Total funds:	N/A
Sectors:	Technology, communications and services

Summary: Ion Equity is a leading corporate finance firm and private equity investor with offices in London and Dublin. Through corporate financing they provide high quality funding and M&A solutions to European emerging and mid-market Technology Media and Telecoms (TMT) and services businesses. Their portfolio includes Aran Technologies, MBI buyout of Irish assets of Shell and LBO/MBO of usit NOW. ION does not provide seed capital

Mentor Capital Partners Limited Partnership

Category:	Venture Capital
Contacts:	Mark Horgan, CEO
Tel:	+353 (0) 1 205 9716
Fax:	+353 (0) 1 205 9889
Email:	info@mentorcapital.ie
Web:	www.mentorcapital.ie
Address:	Mentec House, Pottery Road, Dun Laoghaire, Co Dublin
Investment range:	€500,000-2.5M
Total funds:	€16.5M
Sectors:	ICT, microelectronics and software with enabling functionality

Summary: Mentor Capital provides funding to companies who possess core, enabling technology with potential for significant impact on global markets

NCB Ventures Limited

Category:	Venture Capital
Contacts:	Michael Murphy, CEO
Tel:	+353 (0) 1 611 5942
Fax:	+353 (0) 1 611 5987
Email:	patrick.claffey@ncb.ie
Web:	www.ncbdirect.com
Address:	3 George's Dock, IFSC Dublin 1
Investment range:	€125,000-1.25M
Total funds:	€27M

Sectors: General

Summary: The European Investment Fund Enterprise Ireland, Guinness Ireland and Ulster Bank are investor in this fund and investment is directed to SMEs with significant growth potential. NCB whilst minority equity is only taken. Ireland's leading independent securities firm with interests in institutional equities and fixed income, wealth management, corporate finance, private equity, alternative investments and funds listing & specialist securities. Founded over 22 years ago, NCB is owned in the majority by its senior executives and staff. The Quinn Group, which is one of Ireland's largest privately owned companies, has a shareholding of approximately 20 percent.

Viridian Growth Fund

Category:	Venture Capital
Contacts:	Alan Mawson, Chairman
Tel:	+44 (0) 28 9032 6465
Fax:	+44 (0) 28 9032 6473
Email:	info@clarendon-fm.co.uk
Web:	www.clarendon-fm.co.uk
Address:	Clarendon Fund Managers 12 Cromac Place Belfast BT7 2JB
Investment range:	£50,000-300,000
Total funds:	€10M

Sectors: Manufacturing or tradable service SMEs in Northern Ireland

Summary: The fund is supported by private sector investors and managed by Clarendon Fund Managers. The Department of Enterprise, Trade and Investment and the European Investment Bank provide investment with support under the EU Programme for Peace and Reconciliation. The Fund generally works with company management to identify where activity and personnel resources can be strengthened and to ensure the company is focussed on profitable expansion.

Western Investment Fund

Category:	Venture Capital
Contacts:	Gillian Buckley, Investment Manager
Tel:	+353 (0) 94 986 1441
Fax:	+353 (0) 94 986 1443
Email:	info@wdc.ie
Web:	www.wdc.ie
Address:	Dillon House Ballaghadereen, Roscommon
Investment range:	€63,000-317,000
Total funds:	€32M
Sectors:	All sectors

Summary: The fund provides seed and venture capital to new and existing businesses across a range of sectors in the western region. It will also consider MBOs/MBIs. Larger investments are considered on a syndicated basis with other private investors.

Summary

We have provided a guide book of funding sources for entrepreneurs. Different enterprises present different risk profiles to financiers, hence the need for different funding regimes such as grants, debt financing, venture capital and angel funding. Enterprises that do not fit the criteria for one funding regime may well fit another. For example, a solid yet low-growth company may not be suited for venture capital funding but would be better served by a working capital loan to finance its operations. Similarly, a company heavily involved in R&D should target the many R&D grants available rather than apply for debt financing.

In Table 11 we provide an extensive summary of the differences between the different types of funding sought by today's entrepreneurs. The value of certain types of funding over others is differentiated by the entrepreneur's objective for seeking capital, the holding period for capital, and the collateral essential and additional criteria. Table 11 also presents the differentiating factors used to evaluate the different types of funding including the financial impacts of funding (on balance sheet/cash flow), the monitoring system that generally applies, the value added, and finally the exit mechanism for each type of funding.

This guide book has examined the various forms of capital formation for entrepreneurs. Initial consideration was given to bootstrapping and informal investors, where budding entrepreneurs have their best chances of getting funded. The ensuing book chapters move onto explore debt and equity financing in the form of commercial banks, trade credit, accounts receivable financing, factoring and finance companies, and various forms of equity instruments.

Public stock offerings have advantages and disadvantages as a source of equity capital. Although large amounts of money can be raised in short periods of time, the entrepreneur must sacrifice a degree of control and ownership. In addition, different economic systems have vastly diverse and complex regulations that have to be followed.

Private placements are an alternative means of raising equity capital for new ventures. This placement's greatest advantage to the entrepreneur is limited company disclosure and only a small number of shareholders.

In recent years the venture capital market has grown dramatically. Billions are now invested annually to seed new ventures or help fledgling enterprises grow. The individuals who invest these funds are known as venture capitalists. A number of myths that have sprung up about these capitalists were discussed and refuted.

Venture capitalists use a number of different criteria when evaluating new-venture proposals. In the main these criteria focus on two areas:

- The investment potential of the venture

- The entrepreneur.

The evaluation process typically involves four stages:

- Initial screening

- Business plan evaluation

- Oral presentation

- Final evaluation

In recent years "angel" capital has begun to play an important role in new-venture financing. Everyone with money to invest in new ventures can be considered a source for this type of capital. Some estimates put the informal risk capital pool at a level so significant that it could be measured with the Gross Domestic Product (GDP). Entrepreneurs who are unable to secure financing through banks or through public or private stock offerings will typically turn to the informal risk capital market by seeking out friends, associates, and other contacts who may have (or know of someone who has) money to invest in a new venture.

In addition, we have provided a more than eighty telephone numbers and more than one hundred twenty web addresses of potential funders for entrepreneurs on the island of Ireland.

Table 11 Differences among funding types

Differential factor	Bootstrapping	Informal Investment	Debt Financing	Equity Financing	Venture Capital	Angel Funding
Objective	Launch capital	Launch capital	Interest & principal	Share of ownership	Capital gains	Capital gains
Holding Period	Short	Short-to-mid term	Short-to-mid term	Mid-to-long term	Mid-to-long term	Short-to-mid term
Collateral	None (sometimes credit cards)	Often none, or good-will of relations	Yes	No	No	No
Criteria	Faith in entrepreneur	Faith and trust	Interest spread and security	Potential returns on investment	Potential returns on investment	Potential returns on investment
Impact on Balance Sheet	Increase leverage	Increase leverage	Increase leverage	Reduce leverage	Reduce leverage	Reduce leverage
Impact on Cash Flow	Creative acquisition of resources	Interest / principal repayment, sometimes none	Interest/ principal repayment	Dividend payout	Dividend payout	Dividend payout
Monitoring	Monthly accounting	Family or friends over your shoulder	Loan servicing	Employment contacts, Board seat, operational reports	Board seat, operational reports	Management control in day-to-day operations & decision-making
Value Add	Positioning before other financing	Sometimes expertise, contacts	None	Employee expertise, public credibility	Management assistance, strategic alliances	Management assistance, strategic alliances
Exit Mechanism	Repay or re-invest	Repay or re-invest	Principal repayment	IPO, trade sales, buy-back	IPO, trade sales, buy-back	Trade sale, buy-back

Bottom line

Here are the key learnings from this book. If there's one page to memorize and tell others about, this is it.

- There's plenty of money out there but most young firms aren't "investment ready".

- A business plan is important, but it is better to spend money first on marketing, sales and a Web site, if necessary. Venture capitalists and mentors will help you with the business plan anyway; what they want to see is revenue!

- Only one in ten thousand will ever see the inside of a venture capitalist's office. Concentrate on other sources of funding.

- Government money is available but it's sometimes a slog filling out all the forms and doing the reports.

- After you max out your own finances, look to friends, family and other "foolish" investors!

- Get the numbers right, be honest and don't exaggerate or be overly conservative.

- Don't become a tail-wagging dog, when you have unwittingly become reliant on one or two large investors and they start to bark orders at you.

- Less risky cash is preferred to more risky finance

- Investors are interested in the company, don't sell the product, sell the company.

- Investors will look at your business ideas from a much narrower perspective than you.

- When considering IPO activity, think of using the de-coupled approach that provides more flexibility and minimizes market risk thus improving the outcomes of each deal.

Meditations for entrepreneurs

Here are some meditations to relax you and tame your mind. Focusing, is a narrowing of awareness and of purpose.

"Milestones are either stepping stones or millstones; you have to decide for yourself" Austin Darragh, Leo Laboratories

"There is a line in the Sail Ireland song about the narrowest line between the hero and the fool. I'd prefer to walk that line than be a nonentity" Dermot Desmond, CEO National City Brokers and portfolio entrepreneur

"The end is never near. If you get to the end you've had it" Eddie Haughey, Norbrook Holdings (Pharmaceutical)

"I am asked if we do things for altruistic or commercial reasons. I see no conflict...you can't be a philanthropist and be a failure" Alastair McGuckian, Masstock International.

"Historically, family businesses don't survive long...we employ 2,000 people, so we have an obligation not to disrupt the business with family rows".

"Live poor and die rich". Sean Quinn, Quarries, hotels, insurance and industry.

"I don't get a sense of achievement because I am never content with what we have got" Geoff Read, Ballygowan Spring Water Co. Ltd.

Risk is the greatest of all aphrodisiacs. I like the feeling that you can be wrong but I like the odds to be in my favour even if ever so slightly. Once the risk goes out of a project, I lose interest. Risk is not a philosophy, it's an addiction". John Teeling, Cooley Distillery plc and CountyGlen plc.

"We live not in dozens of markets of millions but in millions of markets of dozens". Joe Krause

"A life spent making mistakes is not only more honourable, but more useful than a life spent doing nothing". George Bernard Shaw

"Only those who dare to fail miserably can achieve greatly". Robert Kennedy

"The rich buy assets. The poor only have expenses. The middle class buys liabilities they think are assets". – Robert T. Kiyosaki, author, entrepreneur, investor

"A wise man changes his mind; a fool never will". Spanish proverb

"You see things, and you say, 'Why?' But I dream things that never were, and I say, 'Why not?'" George Bernard Shaw

"I was following a Nowhere Hunch. A real dumb thing to do! Everybody sometimes does it. Even me. And even you. Oh, you get so many hunches that you don't know ever quite if the right hunch is a wrong hunch! Then the wrong hunch might be right!" Dr. Seuss

"The toughest thing about success is that you've got to keep on being a success". Irving Berlin

"Opportunities are usually disguised as hard work, so most people don't recognize them". Ann Landers

"If you think you can, you can. And if you think you can't, you're right". Mary Kay Ash

"The problem with the French is that they don't have a word for entrepreneur". George W. Bush, discussing the decline of the French economy with British Prime Minister Tony Blair.

"Anyone can be innovative if his life depends on it" Akio Morita, Founder Sony

'That some should be rich, shows that others may become rich, and hence is first encouragement to industry and enterprise' Abraham Lincoln (1864)

"Knowing what is does not tell you what could be" Einstein

"The Body Shop revolutionised the worldwide body-care market…with a £2,000 bank loan" Anita Roddick, The Body Shop

"My technical team said it was impossible…12 months later it was achieved and it was a miracle to create!" Michelle Mone, MJM International

Experiential Exercise

Analysing the Funding Sources

For each funding source, write down what the text says about its usefulness for small firms. Then seek out and interview a representative of each source to find out the person's viewpoint of his or her relationship to small firms.

Source	What the Text Says	Source's Point of View
Banks		
Long-term loans		
Short-term loans		
Intermediate-term loans		
Private placement		
Informal investing		
Public offerings (IPO)		
Finance company		
Factor		
Trade credit		
Business angel investors		
Venture capitalist		

Case: Looking for capital to launch a bookstore

When Mary and Tom Lynch opened their bookstore one year ago, they estimated it would take them six months to break even. Because they had gone into the venture with enough capital to keep them afloat for nine months, they were sure they would need no outside financing. However, sales have been slower than anticipated, and most of their funds now have been used to purchase inventory or meet monthly expenses. On the other hand, the store is doing better each month, and the Lynch family are convinced they will be able to turn a profit within six months.

At present, Mary and Tom want to secure additional financing. Specifically, they would like to raise €100,000 to expand their product line. The store currently focuses most heavily on how-to-do-it books and is developing a loyal customer following. However, this market is not large enough to carry the business. The Lynch family feel that if they expand into an additional market such as capitalising on the insatiable interest people have with decorating and improving their homes – Household DIY books. This would allow the Lynch family to develop two market segments that, when combined, would prove profitable. Mary is convinced that 'Household DIY' is an important niche, and she has saved a number of clippings from national newspapers and magazines reporting that people who buy 'Household DIY' books tend to spend more money per month on these purchases than does the average book buyer. Additionally, customer loyalty amongst this group tends to be very high.

The Lynch family own their entire inventory, which has a retail market value of €280,000. The merchandise cost them €140,000. They also have at a local bank a line of credit of €10,000, of which they have used €4,000. Most of their monthly expenses are covered out of the initial capital with which they started the business (€180,000 in all). However, they will be out of money in three months if they are not able to get additional funding.

The owners have considered investigating a number of sources. The two primary ones are a loan from their bank and a private stock offering to investors. They know nothing about how to raise money, and these are only general ideas they have been discussing with each other. However, they do have a meeting scheduled with their accountant, a friend, who they hope can advise them on how to raise more capital. For the moment, the Lunch family are focusing on writing a business plan that spells out their short business history and objectives and explains how much money they would like to raise and where it would be invested. They hope to have the plan completed before the end of the week and take it with them to the accountant. The biggest problem they are having in writing the plan is that they are unsure of how to direct their presentation. Should they aim it at a banker or a venture capitalist? After their meeting with the accountant, they plan to refine the plan and direct it toward the appropriate source.

Questions

- Would a commercial banker be willing to lend money to the Lynch family? How much? Support your answer with evidence from the text.

- Would this venture have any appeal for a venture capitalist? Why or why not?

- If you were advising the Lynch family, how would you recommend they seek additional capital? You may detail reasons from the text to support your answer.

Case: Seeking capital to grow €3 million venture

The Friendly Market is a large urban supermarket. "Friendly's," as it is popularly known, has more sales per square metre than any of its competitors because it lives up to its name. The personnel go out of their way to be friendly and helpful. If someone asks for a particular brand-name item and the store does not carry it, the product will be ordered. If enough customers want a particular product, it is added to the regular line. Additionally, the store provides free delivery of groceries for senior citizens, cheque cashing privileges for its regular customers, and credit for those who have filled out the necessary application and have been accepted into the "Friendly Credit" group.

The owner, Charles Mooney, believes that his marketing-oriented approach can be successfully used in any area of the country. He is therefore thinking about expanding and opening two new stores, one in the northern part of the same city and the other in a city located 50 miles west. Locations have been scouted, and a detailed business plan has been drawn up. However, Charles has not approached anyone about providing the necessary capital. He estimates he will need about €3 million to get both stores up and going. Any additional funding can come from the current operation, which throws off a cash flow of about €100,000 monthly.

Charles feels two avenues are available to him: debt and equity. His local banker has told him the bank would be willing to look over any business plan he submits and would give him an answer within five working days. Charles is convinced he can get the bank to lend him €3 million. However, he does not like the idea of owing that much money. He believes he would be better off selling stock to raise the needed capital. Doing so would require him to give up some ownership, but this is more agreeable to him than the alternative.

The big question now is, How can the company raise €3 million through a stock offering? Charles intends to check into this over the next four weeks and make a decision within eight weeks. A number of customers have approached him over the past year and have asked him if he would consider making a private stock offering. Charles is convinced he can get many of his customers to buy into the venture, although he is not sure he can raise the full €3 million this way. The other approach he sees as feasible is to raise the funds through a venture capital company. This might be the best way to get such a large sum, but Charles wonders how difficult it would be to work with these people on a long-term basis. In any event, as he said to his wife yesterday, "If we're going to expand, we have to start looking into how we can raise more capital. I think the first step is to identify the best source. Then we can focus on the specifics of the deal".

Questions

- What would be the benefits of raising the €3 million through a private placement? What would be the benefits of raising the money through a venture capitalist?

- Of these two approaches, which would be best for Charles? Why?

- What would you recommend Charles do now? Briefly outline a plan of action he can use to get the financing process started.

Other sources of support and information

Books

- Cooney, T and Hill, S (2002) *New Venture Creation in Ireland*. Oak Tree Press: Dublin.

- Immink, R and O'Kane, B (2003). *Growing Your Own Business*. Oak Tree Press: Dublin – workbook on how to finance a developing business see also www.spotcheckonline.com

- Kenny, I (1991). Out On Their Own. Conversations with Irish Entrepreneurs. Gill and Macmillan: Dublin.

- O'Kane, B (2001). *Starting a Business in Ireland*. Oak Tree Press: Dublin.

- Brierty, V and Kinsella, R (2003). Ireland and the Knowledge Economy. The New Techno-Academic Paradigm. Oak Tree Press: Dublin.

Web resources

- The Irish Venture Capital Association – www.ivca.ie

- The British Venture Capital Association – www.bvca.co.uk

- The European Venture Capital Association – www.evca.com

- The Institute of Directors Northern Ireland – www.iod.com

- The Institute of Directors Ireland – www.iodireland.ie

- Office of the Director of Corporate Enforcement – www.odce.ie

- Ireland Local Authorities – www.irlgov.ie

- Northern Ireland Local Authorities – www.ukonline.gov.uk

- European Patent Office: www.european-patent-office-org

- World Intellectual Property Organisation: www.wipo.int

- Irish and Small and Medium Enterprises Association –www.isme.ie

- Irish Statistical Association – www.istat.ie

- Northern Ireland Statistics and Research Agency – www.nisra.gov.uk

- Institute of Public Administration – www.ipa.ie

- HM Revenue & Customs (HMRC) – www.hmce.gov.uk

- Ireland's Inland Revenue – www.revenue.ie

- General Business Advice – www.clearlybusiness.com

- Business Advice for Irish SMEs – www.growingabusinessinireland.com

- *Entrepreneur* Magazine – www.entrepreneur.com

- Ireland Business Magazine, Business Plus Online – www.bizplus.ie

- Start a Business Programme – www.sabp.co.uk

- Advice for small business – www.thisismoney.co.uk

Glossary of key terms and concepts

Accounts receivable: money that is owed to a company by a customer for products and services provided on credit. Treated as a current asset on a balance sheet.

Barter: a form of trade where goods or services are exchanged for a certain amount of other goods or services, i.e. there is no money involved in the transaction.

Bootstrapping: starting a new business without start-up finance. Bootstrapping alludes to a German legend about a Baron Münchhausen, who was able to lift himself out of a swamp by pulling himself up by his bootstraps.

Build-out allowances: in a lease contract, the landlord will sometimes give an amount to the tenant to build-out the premises.

Business angel: a private investor who contributes money and experience to early stage investments.

Capital gain: the profit realized when a capital asset is sold for a higher price than the purchase price.

Capital structure: the mix of the various types of debt and equity capital maintained by a firm.

Cash flow: the amount of cash derived over a certain period of time from an income-producing property.

Classic venture capital: capital invested only in seed, start-up, early, and expansion stage companies.

Collateral: an asset (such as a car or a home) that guarantees the repayment of a loan. The borrower risks losing the asset if the loan is not repaid according to the terms of the loan contract.

Common stock: represents part ownership of a company. Holders of common stock have voting rights but no guarantee of dividend payments.

Consignment: The consignor retains title to the goods until the consignee has sold them. The consignee sells the goods, collects the commission due and remits the net proceeds to the consignor.

Convertible debentures: loans to a company made by investors, as opposed to loans raised from a bank. The investors receive a fixed rate of interest. Debentures may be "convertible" into shares or "redeemable" for cash at a specified future date.

Corporate angels: Typically, so-called corporate angels are senior managers who have been laid off with generous severances or have taken early retirement.

Debt financing: financing in which you get a loan and go into debt. You are obligated to repay the loan at a predetermined interest rate.

Disclosure: information relevant to specific transactions that is required by law.

Dividend: cash, shares of stock or other assets from a company's profits distributed to stockholders, an equal amount for each share of stock owned.

Due diligence: a process undertaken by potential investors to analyze and assess the desirability, value, and potential of an investment opportunity.

Early stage financing is provided to companies that have completed the product development stage and test marketing as well, but require additional financing to expand commercial manufacturing and sales.

Entrepreneurial angels: The most prevalent type of investor is an entrepreneurial angel. Most of these individuals own and operate highly successful businesses.

Entrepreneur: An individual who organizes and manages labour, capital, and natural resources to produce goods and services to earn a profit, but who also runs the risk of failure

Equity capital: capital, such as shares (or stock), supplied to a firm by shareholders; the returns received by the shareholders are not guaranteed but depend on how well the firm does

Equity financing: provision of funds for capital or operating expenses in exchange for capital stock, stock purchase warrants and options in the business financed, without any guaranteed return, but with the opportunity to share in the company's profits.

Exit strategy: methods by which the initial investors in a company can liquidate their investment in it. The two most common exit strategies are either to take the company public by an initial public offering (IPO) or to sell the company to another firm.

Expansion financing is provided when the start-up company is poised to grow rapidly.

Factoring: process of purchasing commercial accounts receivable (invoices) from a business at a discount.

Feasibility study: combination of a market study and an economic analysis that provides an investor with knowledge of both the environment where a project exists and the expected return on investment to be derived from it.

Finance company: a business that offers short-term loans at substantially higher rates of interest than banks

Franchise: an independent business (the franchisee) sells or markets the products and/or services of a larger firm (the franchisor). The franchisee receives training and marketing support from the franchisor and pays a fee for ongoing support.

Global Entrepreneurship Monitor (GEM): flagship entrepreneurship research project run by London Business School. www.gemconsortium.org

Hire purchase: the right to purchase an asset by the user of the asset according to a pre-agreed method. The user may be the owner for tax purposes.

Informal investors: the 4F's—Friends, Family, Founders and other "Foolhardy investors" (to that we could also add neighbours, work colleagues, and even strangers)

Initial public offering (IPO): The flotation of a private company on a stock exchange.

Interest: a fee charged for the use of money.

Investment banker: the firm acting as an underwriter of an issuer. The investment banker is the conduit between the issuer and the public investors.

Late-stage funding refers to the pre-IPO investments in a company for the purpose of strengthening the positioning of the company, and gaining endorsements from the top venture capital firms as the company prepares for its listing.

Letter of credit: a document, issued by a bank per instructions by a buyer of goods, authorising the seller to draw a specified sum of money under specified terms, usually the receipt by the bank of certain documents within a given time.

Loan servicing: the act of collecting loan payments, handling property tax and insurance escrows, foreclosing on defaulted loans and remitting payments to the investors.

Long-term debt: term loans of one to five years or long-term loans maturing in more than five years.

Management buyout: buyout of a business from its owners by the existing management team running the business.

Market capitalisation: price per share multiplied by the total number of shares outstanding; also the market's total valuation of a public company.

Opportunity cost: cost of a resource, measured by the value of the next-best, alternative use of that resource.

Preferred stock: stock that pays dividends at a specified rate and that has preference over common stock in the payment of dividends and the liquidation of assets.

Principal: the amount of the entire mortgage loan, not counting interest.

Private placement: the underwriting of a security and its sale to a few buyers, usually institutional, in large amounts. No formal prospectus is needed to be prepared in this instance as the buyers are considered to be sophisticated.

Prototype development: the original demonstration model of what is expected to be a series of systems. Prototypes are used to prove feasibility, but often are not as efficient or as well designed as later production models.

Royalty: sum of money paid for the use of a license, or for use of works covered by copyright, patent, registered design or trademark.

Seed-financing: initial funds for a business concept to be developed.

Shareholder: one who owns shares of stock in a corporation or mutual fund.

Stock: an equity or ownership interest in a corporation, measured in shares. Ownership of shares is demonstrated by stock certificates.

Stockholder: any holder of one or more shares in a corporation. A shareholder usually has evidence of being a shareholder; this evidence is represented by a stock certificate.

Trade credit: temporary financing extended by suppliers of goods and services pending the customer settlement.

Trade sale: sale of the equity share of a portfolio company to another company.

Underwriter: a firm, usually an investment bank, which buys an issue of securities from a company and resells it to investors. In general, a party that guarantees the proceeds to the firm from a security sale, thereby in effect taking ownership of the securities.

Value-added: adding value to commodity or product – the ultimate judge of value-added is the consumer. If they will pay more it in the new form it is value-added.

Venture capitalist: Investors who will invest in a company start up for a share of the company.

Vertical integration: an arrangement whereby the same company owns all the different aspects of making, selling, and delivering a product or service.

White knight is someone with better credit who might buy the products and resell them to you for a few percentage points. Also a company, which rescues another that is in financial difficulty, especially one that, saves a company from an unwelcome takeover bid.

Working capital: current assets minus current liabilities. Also called net current assets or current capital.

References

[1] Adapted from: Gwartney, James D., Richard L. Stroup, Russell S. Sobel, and David A. Macpherson. *Economics: Private and Public Choice*, 10th Edition. Thomson/South-Western, 2003.

[2] Albert V. Bruno and Tyzoon T. Tyebjee, "The Entrepreneur's Search for Capital", *Journal of Business Venturing* (winter 1985): 61–74; see also Howard E. Van Auken and Richard B. Carter, "Acquisitions of Capital by Small Business", *Journal of Small Business Management* (April 1989): 1–9.

[3] Jill Andresky Fraser, "How to Finance Anything", *Inc.* (March 1999): 32–48.

[4] Mark Van Osnabrugge and Robert J. Robinson, *Angel Investing* (San Francisco: Jossey-Bass, 2000), p. 37.

[5] Barter Consultants International, "How Barter Works" www.barterconsultants.com/howbarterworks.html

[6] Brush, C.G., Carter, N.M., Gatewood, E.J., Greene, P.G., & Hart, M.M. 2006. The Use of Bootstrapping by Women Entrepreneurs in Positioning for Growth. Venture Capital, 8(1): 15-31.

[7] Carter, R.B., & Van Auken, H. 2005. Bootstrap financing and owners' perceptiosn of their business constraints and opportunities. Entrepreneurship and Regional Development, 17 (March): 129-144. and Van Auken, H. 2005. Differences in the Usage of Bootstrap Financing among Technology-based versus Nontechnology-based firms. Journal of Small Business Management, 43(1): 93-103.

[8] Vadim Kotelnikov, "Bootstrapping: The Most Common Source of Initial Equity for Entrepreneurial Firms" www.1000ventures.com/venture_financing/bootstrapping_methods_fsw.html Other excellent resources include Bill McCready, "Alternative Financing: Venture Capital Is Not The Only Way" : www.business-success-experts.com/articles/bill/billmccready00004.html ; and David Worrell, "Bootstrapping Your Start-up", *Entrepreneur's Start-Ups* magazine, October 2002. www.entrepreneur.com/article/0,4621,303443,00.html

[9] Adapted from Venture Planning Associates, "28 Ways to Finance Your Venture" http://www.ventureplan.com/how.to.finance.your.venture.html

[10] William D. Bygrave with Stephen A. Hunt. (2005). *Global Entrepreneurship Monitor 2004 Financing Report* (London Business School and Babson College) available at www.gemconsortium.org

[11] Paul Reynolds, William D. Bygrave, Erkko Autio and others, *Global Entrepreneurship Monitor: 2003 Executive Report* (Kansas City: Ewing Marion Kauffman Foundation, 2004).

[12] O' Reilly, M., Hart, M (2005). *Global Entrepreneurship Monitor Report Northern Ireland 2005* (Belfast: Invest Northern Ireland) Available at http://www.investni.com/index/about/ab-reports-n-publications/entrepreneurship.htm

[13] Asheesh Advani, "How to Make the Kitchen Table Pitch", *Entrepreneur*, February 7, 2005.

[14] Cliff Ennico, "Accepting Money From Friends & Family", *Entrepreneur*, May 6, 2002.

[15] Multimedia Development Corporation (Malaysia), "Raising Capital" www.technopreneurs.net.my/cms/General.asp?whichfile=&ProductID=20816&CatID=86

16 A complete explanation can be found in Donald M. Dibble, ed., *Winning the Money Game* (Santa Clara, CA: Entrepreneur Press, 1975), 276; see also Bruce G. Postner, "How to Finance Anything", Inc. (February 1993): 54–68.

17 Truls Erikson, "Entrepreneurial Capital: The Emerging Venture's Most Important Asset and Competitive Advantage", *Journal of Business Venturing* 17(3) (2002): 275–290.

18 Ernst & Young "UK Tops the Global League Table for IPOs in 2004". August 2005 http://www.ey.com/global/content.nsf/International/Home

19 With gratitude and acknowledgement to Richard H. Pettway, "IPOs: What we know and what we do not know". March 2004. http://www.business.uts.edu.au/finance/staff/Dick/IPOs-What_we_know_and_do_not_know_012404.pdf

20 David Evanson and Art Beroff, "Burnt Offerings?" *Entrepreneur* (July 1999): 56–59. See also Kenneth W. Clarkson, Roger LeRoy Miller, Gaylord A. Jentz, and Frank B. Cross, *West's Business Law: Legal, Ethical, International, and E-Commerce Environment*, 8th ed. (Mason, Ohio: South-Western/Thomson Learning, 2001).

21 Venture Planning Associates, "Private Placement Memorandums" http://www.ventureplan.com/private.placement.html

22 Triton Foundation, "Raising Finance – Private Placements and Corporate Partnering" www.tritonfoundation.org.au/user/InfoPacks.asp?Key=71

23 Una McCaffrey, "Taking the lunge and making it work", *Irish Times*, 16, Rebruary 2004.

24 See Amitava Guharoy, "Management Buyouts", in International Enterprise Singapore, *Financing Internationalisation: Growth Strategies for Successful Companies* (Singapore: Singapore Information Services, 2004: 144-148) ISSN: 0219-970X www.iesingapore.com

25 Venture capital data are derived from the European Venture Capital Association 2005 Yearbook, the National Venture Capital Association 2005 Yearbook, and data from national venture capital associations.

26 W. Keith Schilit, "How to Obtain Venture Capital", *Business Horizons* (May/June 1987): 78.

27 Adapted from Paul DeCeglie, "The Truth about Venture Capital", *Business Start-Ups* (February 2000): 40–47.

28 John Hall and Charles W. Hofer, "Venture Capitalists' Decision Criteria in New Venture Evaluation", *Journal of Business Venturing* (January 1993): 37.

29 Dean A. Shepherd, "Venture Capitalists' Introspection: A Comparison of 'In Use' and 'Espoused' Decision Policies", *Journal of Small Business Management* (April 1999): 76–87; and "Venture Capitalists' Assessment of New Venture Survival", *Management Science* (May 1999): 621–632.

30 Ronald J. Hustedde and Glen C. Pulver, "Factors Affecting Equity Capital Acquisition: The Demand Side", *Journal of Business Venturing* (September 1992): 363–374.

31 Harry J. Sapienza, "When Do Venture Capitalists Add Value?" *Journal of Business Venturing* (January 1992): 9–28.

32 B. Elango, Vance H. Fried, Robert D. Hisrich, and Amy Polonchek, "How Venture Capital Firms Differ", *Journal of Business Venturing* (March 1995): 157–179; and Dean A. Shepherd and Andrew L. Zacharakis, "Venture Capitalists' Expertise: A Call for Research into Decision Aids and Cognitive Feedback", *Journal of Business Venturing* 17(1) (2002): 1–20.

33 Marie-Jeanne Juilland, "What Do You Want from a Venture Capitalist?" (32) August 1987 issue of *Venture, For Entrepreneurial Business Owners & Investors*, Venture Magazine, Inc., 521 Fifth Ave., New York, NY 10175-0028.

[34] Sohl J. and Sommer B. *Angel Investment Activity: Funding High-Tech Innovations* (2000). Cited in Infometrics Ltd, *New Zealand's Angel Capital Market: The supply side*. A report prepared for New Zealand Ministry of Economic Development, June 2004; Gullander S and Napier G. *Handbook in business angel networks – The Nordic case*, Stockholm School of Entrepreneurship, 2003. Cited in Infometrics Ltd, *New Zealand's Angel Capital Market: The supply side*. A report prepared for New Zealand Ministry of Economic Development, June 2004. Available at http://www.med.govt.nz/templates/MultipageDocumentTOC____1037.aspx

[35] Colin Mason and Richard T. Harrison, "The Size of the Informal Venture Capital Market in the United Kingdom", *Small Business Economics* 15(2) (2000): 137-148.

[36] William E. Wetzel, Jr., as quoted by Dale D. Buss, "Heaven Help Us", *Nation's Business* (November 1993): 29.

[37] William E. Wetzel, Jr., "Angel Money", *In-Business* (November/December 1989): 44.

[38] William E. Wetzel, Jr., "Angels and Informal Risk Capital", *Sloan Management Review* (summer 1983); see also John Freear, Jeffrey E. Sohl, and William E. Wetzel, Jr., "Angels and Non-angels: Are There Differences?" *Journal of Business Venturing* (March 1994): 109–123.

[39] Mark Van Osnabrugge and Robert J. Robinson, *Angel Investing* (San Francisco: Jossey-Bass, 2000), 111.

[40] Vadim Kotelnikov, "Advantages and Disadvantages of Business Angels" http://www.1000ventures.com/venture_financing/ba_pros_and_cons.html

[41] David R. Evanson, *Where to Go When the Bank Says No* (Bloomberg Press, 1998: 40–44).